ANTARCTICA

The Heart of the World

Coral Tulloch

ENCHANTED LION BOOKS
New York

First American Edition published in 2006 by
Enchanted Lion Books, 45 Main Street, Suite 519, Brooklyn, NY 11201

First published in Australia in 2003 by
ABC Books for the Australian Broadcasting Company

A CIP record is on file with the Library of Congress

ISBN 1-59270-054-3

Edited by Lisa Riley
Designed by Patricia Howes
Illustrated by Coral Tulloch
Cover photography:
Elephant Seals, Dr Barbara Smith; Ice Edge, Michael Lunney;
Love Heart, Coral Tulloch; Pancake Ice, Kate Kiefer;
Huskies, Rynill Collection AAD;
Ceremonial South Pole, Dr Tony Press AAD;
Phytoplankton, Professor Harvey Marchant;
Sea Floor, Andrew Tabor (Fishbuster).

Set in Baskerville and Antique Olive by Patricia Howes

Colour separations by Graphic Print Group, Adelaide
Printed and bound in Malaysia by Tien Wah Press

MY JOURNEY

I was extremely privileged to travel to Antarctica under ANARE (Australian National Antarctic Research Expeditions), with the Australian Antarctic Division. Traveling over the Southern Ocean in the scientific and resupply vessel RSV *Aurora Australis* and into Antarctica's icy fringes, I collected material for this children's book.

I was on a resupply voyage to the three Australian Antarctic stations of Mawson, Davis and Casey, and to the subantarctic Macquarie Island. I drew and painted till my cabin was full. I wrote and interviewed and took rolls of photographs. However, like many others, I spent much of my time on the deck of the ship, watching the changing ocean — our passage through and entrance to this unique continent.

Antarctica is so different from any place I have experienced before. My perceptions and my ways of understanding and describing the life around me — all were changed. Antarctica's enormous size and power are humbling. Everyone seemed to feel this. Perhaps this is why Antarctica creates such a bond between the people who have been there.

Many artists have visited Antarctica to bring home their ideas and experiences to others. Whether that be in music, in sculpture, in images or in verse, we all are very fortunate to be able to share with you a glimpse of this extraordinary part of our world.

I have compiled the material for this book not only from my journey south, but with the help and knowledge of the many people who make up the Antarctic family I have been fortunate to meet. This book can be the beginning of your Antarctic journey.

You can read more about my Antarctic voyage at:
www.aad.gov.au/information/aboutantarctica/diaries/stayer/voyage.asp

For great worksheets and a game on the Antarctic Environment, go to:
www.aad.gov.au/classroom/worksheets

This book is dedicated to the following very special people without whose constant encouragement and friendship this book would not have been created.

To Phillipa Foster for her inspiration and her love of all things Antarctic.

To Elizabeth Windschuttle for her passionate idealism and unselfish patronage.

To Peter Boyer for his continued enthusiasm and encouragement that allowed me the freedom to realize a dream.

RSV *Aurora Australis* in the ice.

CONTENTS

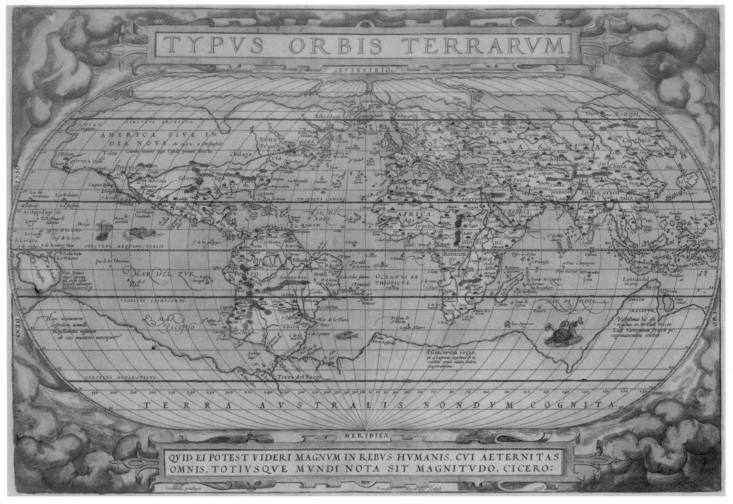

An early world view showing the great unknown land of the south. Abraham Ortelius, *Typus Orbis Terrarum,* Antwerp, 1570. From the Nan Kivell Collection, National Library of Australia.

The ancient Greeks believed that there must be a land to the south that would balance all the known lands of the north. They called it *Antarktikos*, the opposite of *Arktos* (meaning "the bear"), the constellation of stars that lies above the Northern Hemisphere.

People dreamed of this great southern land, still to be discovered. Would it hold new and exotic plants and animals, fruits, spices and mineral wealth? What would the people who lived there be like? But this land was very different to the floating ice of the Arctic or any of the known lands of the north. This massive continent of the south, covered in its weighty sheet of ice, was far more than they could have imagined.

As sailors ventured further south they met with the barrier of an icy ocean. Sails, riggings and flesh froze, but some made it through to tell the tale of what lay beyond the known world. As reports

returned, some came south to claim new territories and to hunt wildlife. Some chased dreams of adventure and science.

But science became the major human endeavor in this land, as without it no one could have sailed through Antarctica's frozen ocean to wonder at its majestic shores. And fortunately we have the legacy and continuance of science that has both protected Antarctica and given us the knowledge of its immense importance. For without Antarctica, life on Earth would be completely different.

Antarctica is the highest, driest, windiest, coldest, cleanest, most isolated and most peaceful continent on Earth. It is a continent of wilderness.

To enter into Antarctica is to enter into a powerhouse of the Earth. The vast Southern Ocean swirls around Antarctica and spreads its waters outwards, refreshing the oceans of the world. The Ocean's surface freezing to double Antarctica's size

in winter and melting to its fringes in summer follows an annual cycle, beating like the pulse that runs through all life, like the heart of our Earth. Its ice sheet is constantly growing and moving, while raging winds flow out from its high plateau like the breath of Earth, the very lungs of our world.

Antarctica's enormous size and energy, its great and rare beauty, are overwhelming for most of us who live a life so removed from this. We can only come to visit Antarctica. We are not natural to this environment. It is harsh and difficult and foreign to us; and we have had to learn how to survive there. Nowhere else in our world do countries work together in true cooperation. In this extraordinary place, the seventh continent, all war and any sort of military presence are banned.

There are threats to Antarctica from human greed. Some countries wish to exploit its wildlife, catching krill and fish. Some countries continue to hunt whales, even in the sanctuary of the Southern Ocean. Any human presence could cause damage and any threat to Antarctica concerns us all.

Antarctica is the only place on Earth that does not belong to one nation. It belongs to everyone. The whole world is responsible for taking care of this most precious continent. Its future lies with us all.

Snow petrels soar above an awe-inspiring Antarctic iceberg.

This NASA sea surface elevation survey map shows a very modern view of the world.

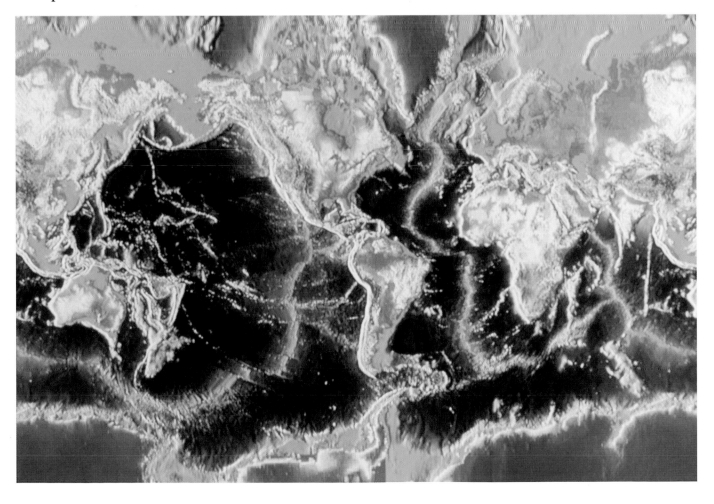

ANTARCTICA'S HISTORY

Our Earth is a beautiful planet. Deep blue oceans and swirling clouds circle the globe, broken only by large, orange-colored masses of land, the continents. But one continent, called the seventh continent, stands out from all the others, with its skin of ice reflecting the sun's light: this is Antarctica.

GONDWANA

Antarctica wasn't always covered in ice. It was once part of a great landmass, called Gondwana. About 160 million years ago, forces within the Earth caused the Earth's crust to start to fracture. Over millions of years Gondwana broke apart. The lands we now call Africa, South America, Australasia and India, with Antarctica as the centre, drifted away from each other. This process, called continental drift, left Antarctica isolated as an island continent at the southern end of the Earth.

Antarctica was also once covered in forests, and benefited from the warm ocean currents that travelled south along the lands of Gondwana. When Antarctica became isolated it was then surrounded by a continuous flow of ocean, which began to cool rapidly. Temperatures dropped and the forests disappeared as Antarctica's land became covered in snow and eventually the snow compressed to ice.

EARTH'S PLACE IN SPACE

Seasons vary throughout the world, but in Antarctica (which surrounds the South Pole) and the Arctic (which surrounds the North Pole) there are two main seasons, summer and winter. There are short periods between the seasons when they have both day and night, but they both experience long periods of darkness in winter and constant light in summer.

NASA image of Antarctica as seen from space. Using red to indicate height, Antarctica here, looks like the heart of our world.

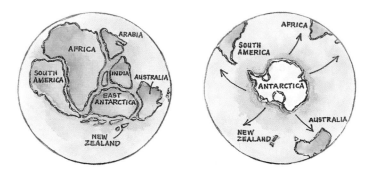

The diagram on the left shows the continents as the land mass Gondwana. The diagram on the right shows the position of Antarctica today.

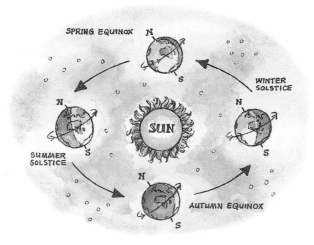

The Earth's orbit around the Sun, showing the seasons.

Tilted at an angle, the Earth rotates on its axis in its orbit around the Sun. It has an elliptical orbit and the South Pole is closer to the sun in its summer than the North Pole is in the northern summer. During the southern summer, Antarctica is always showing its face to the sun and receives more radiation (light and heat) from the sun than the Equator does. But radiation from the sun comes to Antarctica on a low, slanting angle. Falling in a wide band, the heat is spread out. Most of the sun's heat is not absorbed by the continent, but is reflected back into space by the white ice and snow of Antarctica's surface. In winter, Antarctica is turned away from the sun and is in constant darkness.

ANTARCTICA'S HIDDEN HISTORY

Although so much of the land of Antarctica is hidden underneath its ice sheet, a small amount remains ice free and shows us a history of Antarctica's past. In the rocky outcrops, sedimentary layers can be seen that tell of the geological movement and creation of the land of Antarctica. Some ice-free areas contain mineral and fossil deposits that are similar or match those found on other southern continents. These finds support the theory that the southern continents were once joined together as the super continent of Gondwana.

Notes from a geologist
Geology: The study of the composition, structure and history of the Earth, and the processes occurring within it.

Dr. Doug Thost:
"I have always loved being outdoors, looking at and experiencing the world around me. As a geologist I have been fortunate enough to visit some of the most wonderful and exotic places on Earth.

"Through geology you see the world differently. The folds, faults and melting reveal a history of the Earth in the structure of the rocks.

"My interest in Antarctica just evolved. Antarctica is great for a geologist because you can see the rock so much clearer than anywhere else. There are no trees, soils or grasses in your way. The rock thrusts up from the ice to reveal the bare structure of the Earth.

"It is what I'd imagine it would be like going to another planet, as it is alien to everything we experience in our everyday life. It is powerful and humbling and at the same time it can have both great beauty and aggression.

"Using photography, I love making images of the landscape and in Antarctica the landscape makes you fully aware that you are a part of it too."

Big Ben on Heard Island is an active volcano.

Twelfth Lake: Dolerite rock strata (formed as lava moved through narrow cracks) resembles the Roman numerals for 12.

Coal seam in the Prince Charles Mountains. Most minerals are hidden in rock under the ice.

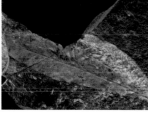

Fossilised fern (*Glossopteris* genus), which is 250 million years old, found in West Antarctica.

Fossilised molluscs (shellfish), which are 170 million years old, found in the Antarctic peninsula.

Site of a find of dolphin bones in West Antarctica, 4.1–4.5 million years old.

Reconstructed bones from the site (at left) reveal a dolphin skull.

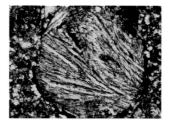

Magnified section through a meteorite. The geology of space can be studied from meteorites. They can be found easily in Antarctica as they fall on snow and ice.

BENEATH THE ICE

The continents of the Earth are part of great slabs, or plates of land on the Earth's surface, known as the Earth's crust. These plates are actually in constant movement. Geologists can now measure directly the movements between continents. Australia's northward movement from Antarctica is approximately 2 1/3 inches a year. At different times through Earth's history, violent movement has taken place. Pieces of the crust have collided and, under pressure of the land being forced together or torn apart, rock beds have buckled. Raised and thrust upwards, they became mountain ranges. Some of these mountains were once the bed of the ocean floor.

We know very little of the detail of the geology of Antarctica because less than 1 percent of its surface is clear of ice. However, the Transantarctic Mountains, which form a divide between East (Greater) and West (Lesser) Antarctica, have given us some of the best clues to Antarctica's geological history — that is, what the Earth is made of, what it looks like and how it moves at various times in history. This mountain range, covering more than 1,367 miles, has many peaks over 13,000 feet high. Most of Antarctica's mountains are buried in ice, with just their peaks visible. These are called "nunataks," an Inuit word meaning "lonely stone."

THE ICE SHEET

The ice that covers the land of Antarctica is called the ice sheet. Imagine Antarctica as a giant cake, bigger than the continent of Australia, with layers of icing continuously being poured over it for hundreds of thousands of years.

The ice sheet is constantly changing and moving. It forms as snow crystals fall and pile on top of each

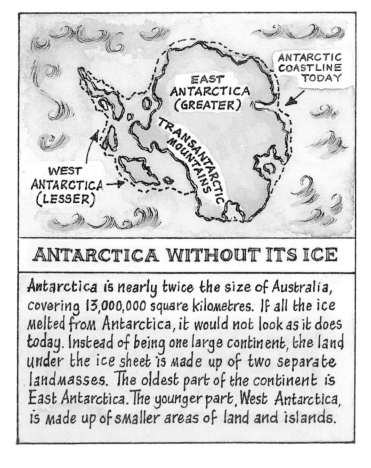

ANTARCTICA WITHOUT ITS ICE

Antarctica is nearly twice the size of Australia, covering 13,000,000 square kilometres. If all the ice melted from Antarctica, it would not look as it does today. Instead of being one large continent, the land under the ice sheet is made up of two separate landmasses. The oldest part of the continent is East Antarctica. The younger part, West Antarctica, is made up of smaller areas of land and islands.

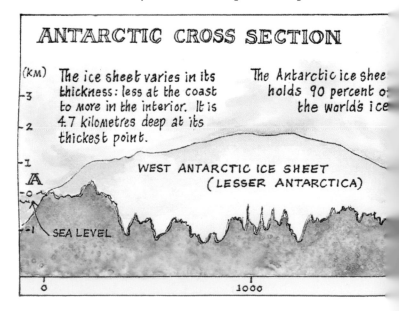

ANTARCTIC CROSS SECTION

(KM)
The ice sheet varies in its thickness: less at the coast to more in the interior. It is 4.7 kilometres deep at its thickest point.

The Antarctic ice sheet holds 90 percent of the world's ice

WEST ANTARCTIC ICE SHEET (LESSER ANTARCTICA)

SEA LEVEL

other, creating a huge weight that compresses the snow below it into ice. This heavy weight places pressure on the ice, which is forced to move down and across the land, flowing from the high interior of Antarctica to the coast. Near the edge of the continent, ice is channelled into streams, which form great rivers of moving ice called glaciers. Pushing through to the coast, glaciers can also flow out over the ocean creating ice shelves, which are frozen to the land but float upon the ocean.

With the push of the ice sheet and the pounding ocean, pieces of the floating ice shelves eventually break off and become icebergs. Some become grounded near the coast and create spectacular guardians to the continent. They can vary in size and shape but some icebergs could fit a city on their back and can take years to melt as they float in the Southern Ocean.

Notes from a glaciologist
Glaciology: The study of the movement and creation of glaciers and ice sheets.

Dr. Barbara Smith:
"If you told me when I was young at school that one day I'd be jumping in and out of helicopters with ice cores in Antarctica, I wouldn't have believed you! I thought that getting to Antarctica was only for the elite few. But I've been there now and had the most exciting time of my life.

"Imagine flying in a helicopter over Antarctica. The breathtaking scenery and the staggering beauty of the landscape have been seen by very few people before, if anyone at all. It's an awesome feeling. Glaciologists working in Antarctica experience this as part of their job! I feel I am one of the luckiest people on Earth.

"Being a glaciologist is fascinating. On the one hand you could be flying out over the vast white emptiness of Antarctica, or you could be in a freezer room cutting up ice for analysis and interpreting the results. But the most exciting thing for me is that you learn how the ice sheet moves, grows and shrinks over time and that you are taking part in ground-breaking research into how our climate is changing and how that can affect our lives."

Ice cliffs at the edge of ice shelves break away to form icebergs.

FACT: Lambert Glacier, in East Antarctica, is the world's largest glacier. It is about 25 miles wide and 248 miles long. It drains nearly 8 percent of Antarctica's ice sheet into the floating Amery Ice Shelf.

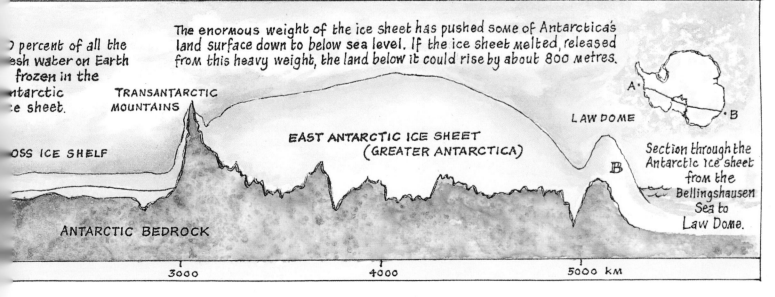

) percent of all the esh water on Earth frozen in the ntarctic e sheet.

The enormous weight of the ice sheet has pushed some of Antarctica's land surface down to below sea level. If the ice sheet melted, released from this heavy weight, the land below it could rise by about 800 metres.

TRANSANTARCTIC MOUNTAINS

LAW DOME

A

B

EAST ANTARCTIC ICE SHEET (GREATER ANTARCTICA)

OSS ICE SHELF

B

Section through the Antarctic Ice sheet from the Bellingshausen Sea to Law Dome.

ANTARCTIC BEDROCK

3000   4000   5000 KM

CONTINENTAL ICE

The ice that has built up on the continent of Antarctica is called continental ice. The ice sheet is not just a flat, solid mass. It is dynamic and changing and some of its varied characteristics are described and illustrated below.

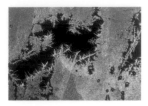

Ice crystals Snow crystals appear in a never-ending variety of shapes and sizes, but are always six sided. Ice crystals form into wonderful shapes.

Hoarfrost is created when ice crystals form and freeze on fallen snow. As the sun hits the ice crystals, they glow like millions of diamonds.

Sastrugi is the name given to sculptured snow that looks like waves. This is caused when the wind blows the snow across the landscape and when it cuts into fallen snow.

Firn As snow falls it compresses into "firn." This can extend from 150 - 200 feet between the snow and the solid ice. Here firn is cut into blocks at Vostok station.

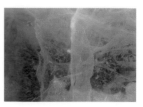

Blue ice is solid ice, and is seen when there is no covering of snow or firn. It is old continental ice that has flowed from inland to the coast and been exposed by erosion.

Crevasse A crevasse, here showing its interior of blue ice, can become covered by falling snow, which makes a bridge across its top. This is dangerous as the crevasse beneath cannot be seen.

Frozen lakes Antarctica has lakes, some deep below the ice. There are also lakes in some ice-free areas like the Vestfold Hills. Some freeze, but others contain the saltiest water in the world, up to 13 times that of seawater, and so they never freeze.

Ice cliffs When ice and firn move down to the ocean they can form great cliffs. In the cliffs of ice shelves you can clearly see accumulated layers of snow compressed to ice through the years.

Glacier A glacier is a moving river of ice. As glaciers move across the land, they are under stress and great cracks and caverns appear in them.

Moraine, which is earth and rocks, can become trapped within the ice sheet. As the ice sheet moves this material is left behind where melting occurs.

Aerial view of crevassed bergs taken at Larsemann Hills, East Antarctica.

Snow is pushed into balls of ice by the wind.

Ice cliff.

Taking a core of the ice gives us valuable and reliable information about the Earth's history. An ice core is like frozen time. As ice forms air is trapped, which can tell us about our Earth's past atmosphere. It also traps any impurities, like dust or chemicals (such as aerosols). Snowfalls can be distinguished between winter and summer and these annual layers can be counted. As scientists date an ice core, they count down its column like counting the years on tree rings.

An ice core.

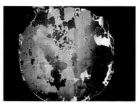

Thin section of an ice core, showing individual ice crystals in polarised light. The colors indicate the crystal orientations. Using this information glaciologists can understand how the Antarctic ice sheet forms.

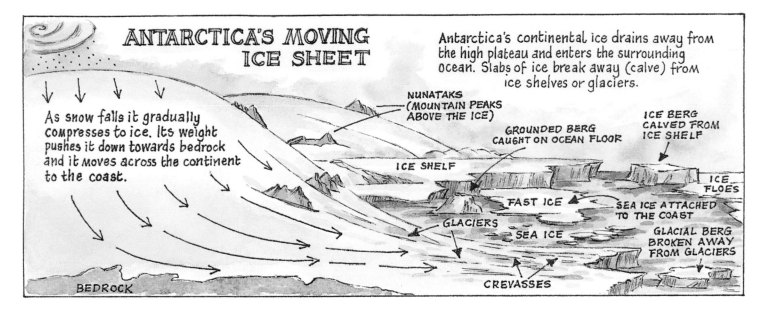

ANTARCTICA'S MOVING ICE SHEET

Antarctica's continental ice drains away from the high plateau and enters the surrounding ocean. Slabs of ice break away (calve) from ice shelves or glaciers.

As snow falls it gradually compresses to ice. Its weight pushes it down towards bedrock and it moves across the continent to the coast.

NUNATAKS (MOUNTAIN PEAKS ABOVE THE ICE)

GROUNDED BERG CAUGHT ON OCEAN FLOOR

ICE BERG CALVED FROM ICE SHELF

ICE SHELF

ICE FLOES

FAST ICE

SEA ICE ATTACHED TO THE COAST

GLACIERS

SEA ICE

GLACIAL BERG BROKEN AWAY FROM GLACIERS

BEDROCK

CREVASSES

SEA ICE

The ice that forms on the continent is very different from the ice that forms on the ocean. As the ocean surrounding Antarctica lives through its annual cycle of freezing and melting, close to the continent there are areas of fast ice and polynas. Fast ice is sea ice frozen to the continent that can build up over the years. Polynas are areas of open water. Cold winds from the continent instantly freeze the water's surface, forming sea ice. The polyna is kept open as the winds force this newly formed ice away. Polynas are continuous ice factories.

The Inuit people of Canada and Greenland have many names for the various ways in which snow falls and forms. But there are no native people of Antarctica, so many of the names that we have to describe sea ice come from countries in the Northern Hemisphere. So that all the peoples of the world can understand, internationally agreed upon codes and symbols have been created for recognizing the formation, movement and decay of sea ice. There also are illustrated dictionaries that serve as a guide to the ice of the oceans and how it behaves, so that people can navigate safely through it.

Sunset on an icy ocean.

"In all my travels in more than thirty lands I had seen nothing so simply magnificent as this stupendous work of nature. The grandest and most beautiful monuments raised by human hands had not inspired me with such a feeling of awe as I experienced on meeting with this first Antarctic iceberg."
Herbet G. Ponting, *The Great White South*, 1921

Notes from an ice pilot

Peter Dunbar:
"I have been working at sea for 20 years, but going to Antarctica and driving ships in ice is like going to a different planet. After years of experience of driving ships in ice, I have picked up a wealth of knowledge, but I am still learning every time I go down.

"The conditions of ice and weather are continuously changing and no matter how many times you experience it, it is a different and an exciting adventure each time.

"I have been told for 20 years that the number one rule to driving ships is 'Don't hit anything'. But in an icebreaker, not only do you hit the ice but if you don't break through the first time, you back up and hit it again!

"Antarctica is the coldest, windiest, wildest, most amazing, dangerous, unpredictable, beautiful, frustrating and untamed place on Earth, and I love it with a passion. To top off the whole incredible experience, you also meet some of the best people from all over the world, who have their own amazing stories and experiences to share."

Wild ocean

THE SOUTHERN OCEAN

Antarctica is surrounded by the Southern Ocean. Near the continent, its surface water freezes and melts and is whipped by powerful winds. It is the only ocean that circles the globe without being stopped by land and is one of the roughest and most dynamic oceans in the world. Warm water and warm, moist air from the Pacific, Indian and Atlantic Oceans meet with the cold water and air of the Antarctic at a boundary called the Antarctic Polar Front. (This used to be referred to as the Antarctic Convergence.)

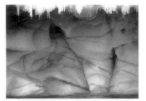
Ice edge

Grease ice

THE CIRCUMPOLAR CURRENT

The Southern Ocean is also home to the longest ocean current in the world, the Circumpolar Current. This flows in an easterly direction and carries 150 times more water around Antarctica than the flow from all of the world's rivers combined. Cold, dense or heavy waters are formed around Antarctica (see diagram below) and sink to the bottom of the ocean. These waters, carried by the Circumpolar Current, spread out into the basins of the Atlantic, Indian and Pacific Oceans. Flowing toward the Equator, they are continuously renewing the world's oceans and have a powerful influence on balancing the Earth's climate.

Bergy bits

Pancake ice

Bergs at sunset

THE FROZEN OCEAN

The ocean's water begins to freeze when the temperature goes below 29°F. As the ice crystals begin to form, they rise to the surface and create an oily-looking layer called "grease ice." As the crystals grow they bump against each other with the water's movement and look like little rounds, called "pancake ice." Water freezes to the ice, snow falls and the pancakes join together creating larger and thicker areas of ice called "floes." Icebergs and fragments of broken icebergs, called "bergy bits" move through the ocean and eventually break down and melt. Some sea ice will remain frozen throughout the year, this is called "old ice" and is built up with snowfalls and new ice freezing to it.

Floes

Tabular berg

Large floes

Jade berg

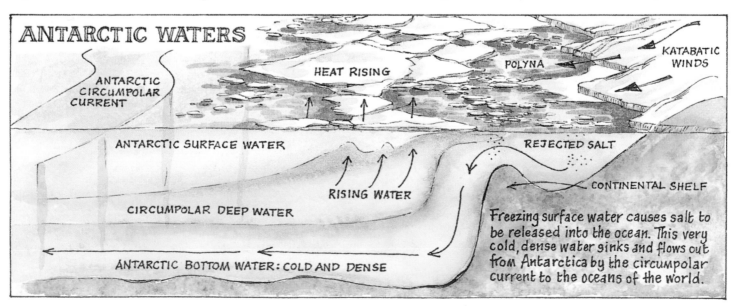

ANTARCTIC WATERS

KATABATIC WINDS

HEAT RISING

POLYNA

ANTARCTIC CIRCUMPOLAR CURRENT

ANTARCTIC SURFACE WATER

REJECTED SALT

RISING WATER

CONTINENTAL SHELF

CIRCUMPOLAR DEEP WATER

ANTARCTIC BOTTOM WATER: COLD AND DENSE

Freezing surface water causes salt to be released into the ocean. This very cold, dense water sinks and flows out from Antarctica by the circumpolar current to the oceans of the world.

Ice crystals, high in the atmosphere, create a halo around the sun.

Approximate sea ice coverage, winter.

Approximate sea ice coverage, summer.

ANTARCTICA'S CLIMATE

Antarctica is the coldest, windiest and driest continent on Earth, surrounded by the stormiest ocean. The atmosphere and the ocean transfer heat and moisture throughout the world and Antarctica plays a vital part in this exchange, affecting global weather patterns.

There are different conditions between the interior, coastal areas and the surrounding ocean. The Antarctic ice sheet rises up, like a dome, high above sea level. This is called the plateau. The highest areas of Antarctica have recorded the lowest temperatures. At Vostok, a Russian station high on the plateau, they recorded a temperature of –129 °F in July 1983. Some areas that are near to or on the coast are called "oases," being dry valleys where no snow falls. There the bare ground absorbs more of the Sun's radiation, and creates warmer temperatures than in other Antarctic areas.

In Antarctica the air is cold and very dry. Many of the world's deserts receive more moisture in a year than is recorded high on the Antarctic plateau. Low pressure systems form in the Southern Ocean and swirl towards the Antarctic coast, bringing heat and moisture with them as they pass over warmer oceans. Most die out before they reach the coast, but some may cause snow to fall.

"When the sun was out there were nearly always mock-suns red gold or prismatic, and always magnificent ... When you gazed upon this strange and awe-inspiring sky you felt as though you had stepped into a world where the laws of Nature, as you had known them, were suspended and over-ruled by some vast Power, which was thus making itself known to you."
Frank Worsley, *Endurance*, 1939

SEASONAL CHANGE

The freezing and melting of sea ice around Antarctica is one of the biggest seasonal changes to happen in the world. In winter, the surface waters freeze and spread out from Antarctica. Larger than the continent itself, this sea ice doubles the size of Antarctica. In summer, the sea ice reduces to a fringe around Antarctica's edges. Water exchanges gases such as oxygen and carbon dioxide with the atmosphere. Only in winter, when the water cools and sinks, can gases be carried into and replenish the deep ocean. This annual cycle of freezing and melting of the surface waters has a large impact on our climate. Sea ice is both a sensitive indicator for climate change and a very important marine habitat.

KATABATIC WINDS

Just as the moving ice sheet drains at the coast through glaciers, strong winds, called katabatics (meaning "down flowing") drain out from Antarctica. Like cold air rushing from an open fridge, the katabatic winds fall from the high plateau to the coast. Winds with the force of tropical cyclones have been recorded and, together with low temperatures, they can cause exposed skin to freeze. Blizzards are common and are a combination of strong wind, freezing temperatures and snow.

Notes from a meteorologist
Meteorology: The study of the phenomena of the atmosphere, especially for weather forecasting.

Steve Pendlebury:
"The Antarctic continent is such an interesting place that there is far too much to record on paper, so we trust our memories to be etched with the wonderment of it all. Firstly, the weather rules. When there are katabatic winds, things are fine if you're inside a heated building listening to the wind howling. But if you have to go outside, like the weather people do to make an observation, then you soon learn about the power of the wind. You can be blown many metres over slippery ice. There are white-outs, when low clouds settle over ice and cover the sun's rays so no shadows can form. You lose all perception of depth and can feel like you're walking in the sky.

"Meteorologists make observations of the clouds, record different weather patterns, temperatures and wind speeds and then report these conditions to weather centers around the world. They predict the weather conditions for safe travel in Antarctica."

LIFE IN ANTARCTICA

All animal and plant life in Antarctica live around the edges of the continent and in its ocean. The vast mass of ice, fierce winds and the extreme cold make living in the interior of Antarctica impossible.

In winter, as the continent is cloaked in darkness and the surface of the ocean freezes to form pack ice, many animals leave Antarctica and its waters. Most small sea life, such as krill, move to greater depths, where the ocean temperatures are more stable. Animals that depend on krill for their main food source, such as some penguins and baleen whales, either switch to fish and squid or migrate north from Antarctica. Only one warm-blooded animal remains on the continent through the cold, dark winter—the Emperor penguin.

ANTARCTIC WINTER

To survive the Antarctic winter, life has evolved and adapted to this environment. Small plants such as algae, lichens and mosses can be found beneath an insulating layer of snow or in tiny cracks in rocks, which provide shelter, light, warmth and moisture. Whales, seals and penguins have developed a thick layer of insulating fat under their skins to protect them from the cold. Some fish contain a substance similar to antifreeze. The feathers of a penguin overlap in layers. They have an oil gland near their tail and, using their bill, they spread this oil on their feathers to make a waterproof surface. Many warm-blooded animals conserve their energies in order to keep their body heat stable.

ANTARCTIC SUMMER

In spring and summer Antarctica bursts with life. The continent is bathed in light and the pack ice begins to break up. This promotes an abundant growth of microscopic life, which provide the energy upon which all Antarctic life depends (see illustration pages 20–21). There is also a frenzy of feeding and breeding. Birds make nests and tend to their eggs and chicks. Seals have pups on sea ice, ice shelves or on the coast. It is a continuing cycle of light and life and of darkness and survival.

UNDER THE ICE

Compared to the vast loneliness of the Antarctic ice sheet, the ocean around Antarctica teems with life. Each drop of water is full of microscopic life, called plankton; a mix of tiny, mainly one-celled plants called phytoplankton, and animal life called zooplankton. Microscopic plants can multiply up to 60 million cells in a quart of water and turn the sea oily, greenish brown and smelly. As they die they are consumed by bacteria and viruses and are food for microscopic animals. They in turn become food for larger animals. From the smallest of organisms to the largest mammal on Earth, the blue whale, the ocean supports the largest of all of the Antarctic communities.

Sediments are carried from the land by glaciers and icebergs. The waters are nutrient and oxygen rich and a wide variety of life survives. Although the ocean surface freezes, water temperature is fairly stable and life has evolved, over time, to exist there.

Below the ice, the underwater world of Antarctica is full of life and color.

A diver beneath the ice.

Notes from a plant ecologist
Plant ecology: *The study of the way in which plants grow in and react to their natural environment.*

Kate Kiefer:
"I was used to working in forests and places where plants were large and there were always lots of trees. I had worked with mosses and lichens before, but nothing could prepare me for what I was about to see in Antarctica.

"There are no large plants, only tiny blobs of mosses hiding under rock and snow, huddled together in places where they can find shelter from the harsh Antarctic winds. The lichens grow on bare rock surfaces. Working outside is extremely difficult. I would often have to use my body to shelter the plants I was looking at, against the harsh wind and flying snow.

"Both Antarctica and the subantarctic Islands have their own very distinctive set of plants which are adapted to coping with the harsh environments they live in. But working there is so much more than looking at plants. In the small community of people, everyone helps each other and you make many special friends. There is pristine wilderness and sometimes the only sounds you can hear are those of birds, or seals and the swirling wind — depending on how Mother Nature is feeling."

UNDER THE MICROSCOPE

Tiny, single-celled organisms called microbes are the most numerous form of life on Earth. In Antarctica they are found in the air, snow, ice, water, and even in the surfaces of rocks. They have been found in lakes that have been trapped beneath the ice sheet for millions of years and in lakes so salty that they never freeze. Microbes even live in the dry valleys, where no rain has fallen for at least two million years. Scientists use powerful microscopes to count, identify and learn about these tiny organisms which play a vital role in shaping the Antarctic and global environment.

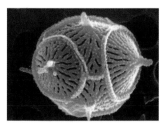

An Antarctic diatom (left), the most common phytoplankton in the Southern Ocean, and parmales (right), single-celled algae, under the Scanning Electron Micrograph. Scale: 1,000 of a millimetre.

Phytoplankton, seen above under the microscope (left) and in an upturned ice floe (right), growing within the ice.

Bacteria and viruses are extremely abundant. Viruses eat the bacteria and help break down what is known as marine snow (see pages 20–21).

Algae can form on snow and ice in the coastal regions and can reproduce in large numbers and cause color changes in the snow such as green, red and orange.

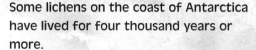

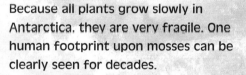

Some lichens on the coast of Antarctica have lived for four thousand years or more.

Because all plants grow slowly in Antarctica, they are very fragile. One human footprint upon mosses can be clearly seen for decades.

Some mosses can survive for years under snow and ice and then, when a thaw occurs, can start growing again.

There are 700 recorded species of aquatic (water) and terrestrial (land) algae found in Antarctica.

Mosses and lichens have adapted to their Antarctic life. Many survive long periods of drought, and snow cover can protect them from the wind and provide moisture.

Lichens grow very slowly in Antarctica and can have growth rates from as little as 1/3 of an inch per 100 years to 1/3 of an inch per 1,000 years.

ANTARCTIC WILDLIFE

These two pages show some of the wildlife of Antarctica:

Krill There are about 85 species of krill. Adult Antarctic krill are approximately 2 1/3 inches in length and weigh about .03 ounces. They swim together in massive swarms, hundreds of feet across and 50-65 feet deep. Thousands of krill can pack each cubic foot of water and the ocean can look orange. They mainly feed on phytoplankton and in turn are eaten by most of the other Antarctic wildlife, from fishes and seabirds to the giant whales.

Southern elephant seal The southern elephant seal is the largest of all the seals of the Southern Ocean. The males can weigh over 4 tons. They feed throughout the Antarctic, but come to breed on the subantarctic islands (see The Subantarctic, pages 40–41).

Emperor penguin These are the largest of all the penguins. As an adult, they can weigh over 80 pounds and are about 3 1/4 feet in height. They breed on the Antarctic coast in winter where the males are left to incubate the egg, huddling together against the winter winds. They can dive deeper (over 3 1/2 miles down) than any bird.

Squid There are different types of squid in the Southern Ocean. They are numerous and provide food for many Antarctic animals. Sperm whales feed on squid, including the giant squid, which lives deep in the ocean, reaching up to 60 feet in length. Its sucker marks are found scarring most of these whales.

Crabeater seal Crabeater seals live exclusively around the pack ice. Despite their name, they mainly eat krill, not crabs, and are the most numerous of all the seal species in the Southern Ocean.

Adélie penguin Adélie penguins spend the winter on the pack ice and return to the same stony breeding grounds and nests each year. They can leap vertically out of the water and onto the ice. This is helpful for escaping their main predator, the leopard seal.

Gentoo (not pictured) **and chinstrap penguins** (right). These penguins also come to the continent of Antarctica, but are found on the peninsula and the subantarctic islands (see The Subantarctic, pages 40–41).

Antarctic ice fish These fish do not have red blood cells. Their blood is almost translucent and they have a ghostly appearance.

Weddell seal Weddell seals live under the fast ice, attached to the continent. In order to breathe, they must come up through cracks and holes in the ice. During winter these cracks can freeze over and so to maintain breathing holes, this seal uses its teeth to open up the ice. They do come out onto the ice to rest, moult and to have their pups.

Seal pup

Leopard seal Leopard seals breed on the pack ice. They eat fish, squid and krill, but favor penguins and some seals. Their teeth are perfect for gripping and tearing at flesh. Once taken, they can flick the skin off an Adélie penguin like a corkscrew of orange peel.

Ross seal (not pictured). Ross seals live mostly on the pack ice. They have very large eyes, which is thought to be a help when catching prey in the darker depths.

Snow petrel The family of petrels are found throughout the world, but are more numerous than the penguins in the Antarctic. Snow petrels are pure white but have a dark down below the feathers, which absorbs the Sun's radiation.

Skua Skuas are related to gulls. They defend their territory aggressively and will raid the nests of other birds, eating eggs and chicks. They will also feast upon carcasses.

WHALES

There are six species of toothed whales and dolphins that come to the waters around Antarctica; these include the killer and sperm whale. The blue, sei, humpback, fin, minke and the southern right whale are all baleen whales. They filter the water for their food through combs of fibrous plates called baleen.

Humpback whale
The humpback whales migrate close to coasts and give birth in shallow waters and so are the whales most often sighted. They are known for their calls or "songs," which scientists believe they use to call to each other through the vast ocean.

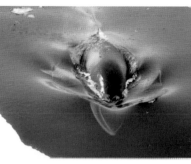

Minke whale Minke whales are small in comparison to most whales. They also feed mainly on krill at the ice edge.

Southern right whale
This whale likes to breed in harbors and bays on its northern migration. Whalers found them easy to catch — once harpooned they would float on the surface — so they were named the 'right' whale to catch.

Killer whale The killer whale is actually a large dolphin and a successful hunter. Its sharp teeth enable it to feast on larger prey such as penguins, seals and even other whales.

Blue whale Like most whales, the blue whale comes to Antarctica as part of its north–south migration. It is the largest animal on Earth and feeds mainly on krill at the ice edge.

"We huddled in the back of a Hagglunds vehicle. As the cab jumped about in the gale force winds, hanging on to the sides in the most severe gusts, we feared we would be rolled over in the winter blizzard. I rubbed a hole in the frosted window and peered into the storm. There they were, barely visable in the drifting snow, three thousand penguins, many with an egg on their feet. Occasionally shuffling a few inches, they shared the windward and coldest side of an enormous huddle to protect the others. Shuffling on, just in time, they would seek shelter in the lee of the next in line. I slumped back, feeling vulnerable and alien, but marvelled at the truly awesome sight of these emperor penguins."
Rob Easther, Station Leader

Notes from a biologist
Biology: The study of the science of living organisms.

Lyn Irvine:
"I work with Adélie penguins off the Antarctic coast. I study the lives, feeding and breeding of these wonderful penguins. My time begins when the penguins arrive on the islands after walking hundreds of miles over the ice to get there. It's exciting to see silent and empty islands transform into energetic worlds of hustle, bustle and noise. Coming to breed, they all arrive within a few days of each other.

"The Adélies fill me with admiration and laughter. Full of character and personality, they are tough and strong, courageous and feisty, but are also comical, clumsy and cute. They can sit through raging blizzards seemingly unconcerned, fast for weeks while incubating their eggs and swim for days to find food for their chicks. Yet, they are clumsy on the ice and slip and slide, they steal each others nesting stones like little thieves, and they get grumpy and moody when they moult.

"The highlight of my work is at Christmas time when the chicks hatch and the colony turns into a sea of whistles. I can't think of a better Christmas present than watching the colony bursting with new life.

"I feel very privileged to live with the penguins in their natural environment. I think I've got the best job in the world. Antarctica to me is Mother Nature at her best — wild, untamable and invincible. There is no other place like it in the world."

In Spring, the pack ice begins to break up and there is a burst of life. Nutrient-rich water and sunlight promote the growth of abundant microscopic plant life (phytoplankton) and animal life (protozoa). These support most other forms of life in Antarctic waters.

Some birds, such as skuas eat penguin eggs and chicks.

Snow algae can grow on melting snow. Mosses and lichens compete for space on bare rock.

Killer whales eat fish, squid, penguins and seals.

Leopard seals eat fish, squid, penguins and seals.

Weddell seals eat fish, squid and crustaceans.

Coastal ice and icebergs can scrape away life on the sea floor.

Kelp forests in the Antarctic and Subantarctic provide shelter and food for some marine life.

Phytoplankton and protozoa form the foundation of the food for krill and other zooplankton.

Some seals live mainly on eating krill.

Life on the sea bed is a rich mix of both animals and plants, providing food and shelter.

zooplankton eat the waste products of others.

Fish eat krill, other zooplankton and each other.

Toothed whales eat squid and a variety of fish.

...rds eat krill, fish and squid.

Penguins eat krill. Some eat other crustaceans, squid and fish.

...ious ...staceans ...er under sea ice ...raze on ...lgae.

...hant ...s dive ...deep ...eat fish ...squid.

Squid eat krill, fish and other squid.

Baleen whales do not have any teeth. They filter their food through bristly plates. They eat krill and other zooplankton.

...etons of ...oscopic life, ...eria and droppings ...animals create ...ne snow. This is ...mportant ...munity of ...anisms and food ...zooplankton.

• Compared to many regions of the world, insects in Antarctica are rare. These include some parasitic lice which gather in birds' nests or feathers and on seals.

• There are inland waters in Antarctica. Some contain layers of both fresh and salt water. Microbes have been found living in lakes, even below the ice.

• Giant petrels are sometimes referred to as "stinkers," because they produce a stinking stream of vomit when they are threatened.

• Penguins, seals and whales have a layer of fat, or blubber, that helps to insulate them from the cold and provides a source of energy when food is scarce.

• Penguins use their flippers to 'fly' under the water. They can move at great speeds and achieve long dives.

• There are many fish species that live in the Antarctic waters. They have a protein in their blood that works like an antifreeze to lower the freezing point of their body fluids.

• The Patagonian toothfish lives deep below the surface waters. It grows very slowly but can live up to 50 years of age and weigh up to 322 pounds.

• Some sponges on the sea floor are larger than a human.

• The wandering albatross can travel thousands of miles, using the wind above the waves as a source of power.

• Male Emperor penguins form a huddle against the winter cold. With an egg on their feet, which they cover with a special layer of fatty skin, they shuffle in turn to rotate in the huddle. The middle of the huddle is very warm, while at the edge it can be freezing cold. By constantly changing position, all the animals can stay warm.

• The southern elephant seal can dive to over 5,000 feet and can stay underwater for up to two hours at a time.

ANTARCTICA'S HUMAN HISTORY

EXPLORATION AND EXPLOITATION

Our first understanding of Antarctica comes mainly from European explorers. The mystery of *Terra Australis Incognita* (meaning the unkown land of the south), excited many explorers to sail beyond known lands.

Besides searching for land to claim as their own, they hoped to find new fruits and spices, plants and animals and valuable minerals such as gold. They returned with many tales of adventure and discovery and made maps of the lands and charts of the seas.

In 1519, the Portuguese explorer Ferdinand Magellan undertook a Spanish voyage and sailed down the coast of South America and into the Pacific Ocean, by way of a strait of water. He believed that the land to the south, Tierra del Fuego, was the great unknown land of the south. The English explorer, Francis Drake, proved Magellan was mistaken when in 1578, Drake was blown from his course and found himself in huge seas beyond Tierra del Fuego. The mysterious land of the south was still to be discovered.

Print of Cook's ship HMS *Adventure* in the ice.

COOK'S VOYAGES

Others tried searching for the mythical continent of *Terra Australis Incognita*, but failed. It was nearly 200 years later that the English Captain James Cook was sent south and became the first to cross the Antarctic Circle. With a fleet of two ships, on a voyage to discover and take possession of the Great Southern Land, he spent three years searching. His fleet circled what we now call Antarctica, but the great floes of sea ice stopped Cook from finding the continent. However, he did prove that this icy realm was not connected to any other on Earth.

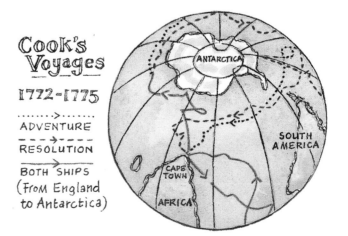

AFRICA

COOK 1772-75

DAVIS 1820-22

AKON VII SEA

CA

BISCOE 1830-32

MAWSON 1911-14

DAVIS SEA

DUMONT D'URVILLE SEA

D'URVILLE 1837-40

AUSTRALIA

ND

Although there were people living in Tierra del Fuego on the tip of South America, we know very little of of their legends, voyages or discoveries further South.

There is a legend that a Polynesian, voyaging further South than any before, was the first to See the icebergs of the Antarctic.

Print of whaling in the Southern Ocean.

WHALERS AND SEALERS

Within ten years of Cook's voyage, hearing stories of the southern wildlife, the first whalers and sealers went south. The hunters killed fur seals for their skins and elephant seals for their blubber. Whales were slaughtered for their blubber (oil from the blubber was used for industry, lighting and medicines), bones and ambergris (a valuable substance used in making perfumes). Penguins were also hunted and their blubber melted down to produce oil.

Many voyages south combined hunting the wildlife with exploration and discovery, as many ships headed into unknown waters. Working from their ships and on the ice floes they also discovered various subantarctic and Antarctic islands.

In search of new harbors and fisheries, the Russian explorer Thaddeus von Bellingshausen sailed around Antarctica and first sighted the continent in 1820. In the same year, British naval officer Edward Bransfield, sent to report on setting up a colony, saw the mountains of the Antarctic Peninsula.

In the 1830s and 1840s various major expeditions from many countries made it through the pack ice to the continent. They made landings and raised the flags of their nations. Their scientific recordings and maps produced a clear picture of Antarctica. They described a continent with some mountainous outcrops, covered by a steely ice sheet: a place where everything froze and in winter there was no light, only constant wind.

So, people believed Antarctica to be a frozen desert: too difficult to mine for its minerals, if any existed; impossible to grow fruits and spices and for any human to survive there. Apart from a British expedition that travelled the world for four years collecting scientific information on the oceans, the only other voyages south for many years were made by whalers and sealers.

Then in 1897, a Belgian naval officer, Adrien de Gerlache, and a team of scientists were the first to camp and travel in Antarctica. Spending the winter on their ship the *Belgica*, they proved that people could survive in the frozen darkness of an Antarctic winter.

THE HEROIC AGE

The first expedition to make a planned winter camp in the Antarctic was the British Antarctic Expedition, also called the *Southern Cross* Expedition. It was funded by British money and headed by a Norwegian, Carsten Borchgrevink. Building huts at Cape Adare in Victoria Land, they raised the British flag, although most of the expeditioners were Norwegians. They gathered significant scientific information, but more importantly they proved that a team could survive living on the continent all year round.

Science on ice.

The *Endurance* crushed by ice. On October 27, 1915, Shackleton's men had to abandon the sinking ship and camp on the ice.

Much was now known about the frozen ocean surrounding Antarctica, but the continent itself remained a barrier. It could only be reached by ship in the short Antarctic summers and even then many ships became trapped in the ice floes and were crushed.

From the beginning of the twentieth century many major expeditions were planned. An increased interest in science and the human desire to explore and win against the elements, saw many nations attempt the hazardous journey south. Claims were staked at the frozen edges of Antarctica and bases were built. Winters could now be spent at a camp, or base, so exploration of the land could continue the following summer.

This photograph, by Herbert Ponting, shows the *Terra Nova* through a grotto in an iceberg.

Unloading supplies.

Workshop, Cape Denison, Commonwealth Bay (Mawson's expedition).

Captain Oates and ponies on the ship *Terra Nova* (Scott's expedition).

In order to explore the land, however, they needed resources. Everything the expedition would need had to be brought aboard the ship: building materials, food, clothing, scientific equipment and animals to help transport it all across the ice. Much had been learned about what was useful from explorations in the Arctic, and so huskies and horses were taken to the continent.

"I can say truthfully that I had forgotten much of the outside world. My sense of values had so readjusted itself that for the time being I was unable to picture an existence in which a desert of ice and snow, battles with sea-leopards, the dread of killer whales, and a regard for penguins as almost personal friends did not play a part."
Frank Worsley, *Endurance*, 1939

Against the blizzard. This photograph, by Frank Hurley, captures the power of a blizzard as one man struggles with an ice pick against its force.

Kitchen duties, Cape Denison, Commonwealth Bay (Mawson's expedition).

The expeditioners themselves needed to be able to carry out many tasks in order to survive. They would also need to provide shelter and friendship for each other during their southern isolation. They created their own small society on the ice.

As many expeditions from different countries headed south, they not only claimed territories for their own countries but undertook important scientific work, which gave the world a greater understanding of this great southern continent. However, many areas were still not mapped and the desire to be the first to reach the South Pole soon turned into a race.

Two years before Amundsen reached the South Pole, a British party located the South Magnetic Pole.

"... when we set forth southward to establish depot number one, we marked the route with bamboo poles, surmounted by flags. We did not have enough flags to mark the entire route, so we resorted to dried fish stuck upright in the snow."
Roald Amundsen,
My Life as an Explorer, 1927

During a British expedition in 1902, Robert Scott, Edward Wilson and Ernest Shackleton made an attempt to reach the South Pole. They were forced to turn back, as their dogs grew fatigued and the men began to suffer from illness. In 1911, two different expeditions set out to reach the Pole: one headed by a Norwegian, Roald Amundsen, the other by Englishman, Robert Scott. Amundsen beat Scott to the Pole by one month and tragically, Scott's party all died on the return trip.

The hardships of the continent took many lives. There are fantastic stories of epic journeys undertaken in Antarctica. Yet at the same time as the race to the Pole was under way, others were continuing in serious scientific work.

Captain Scott in his quarters at the Terra Nova hut, Cape Evans, Ross Island.

"Thursday, March 29th ... I do not think we can hope for any better things now. We shall stick it out to the end, but we are getting weaker, of course, and the end cannot be far. It seems a pity, but I do not think I can write more.
"Last entry. For God's sake look after our people."
Robert Scott, from his diary,
The Antarctic Ocean, 1941

The *Wyatt Earp* in heavy ice floes.   Sea plane (a de Havilland Fox Moth).

Keeping a record of exploration has always been important. Written accounts of daily life and new lands explored are found among the many diaries of explorers. Artists sketched new coastlines, animals and adventures. With the development of photography came some of the most beautiful images of Antarctica. These remain as a poetic memory of the Heroic Age.

Huskies at a camp.

THE ANTARCTIC TREATY

As scientific work continued on the continent and i its ocean, so did the claims for land and territory. In 1957–58, the International Geophysical Year, man countries focused their attention on Antarctica. This was a time when nations were highly suspicious of each other, but they agreed to put aside their differences and political arguments and co-operate to further scientific knowledge in Antarctica. This led to the signing of the Antarctic Treaty in 1959. Signed originally by 12 countries, it is now open to any member of the United Nations.

The Antarctic Treaty is an extraordinary agreement between the world's nations.

"The Treaty provides an example to the world of how nations can successfully work together to preserve a major part of this planet, for the benefit of all mankind."

A NEW HOPE FOR OUR WORLD

"Antarctica is a natural reserve devoted to peace and science."

The Treaty applies to the region south of 60 degrees latitude and states in part:

• Antarctica should always be used for peaceful purposes only and military activities are prohibited on the continent;

• There must be freedom of scientific research throughout Antarctica;

• Any member nation can inspect any other nation's stations and activities; and

• nuclear testing and radioactive waste disposal are banned in Antarctica.

International groups have been set up to help plan the future of Antarctica's resources.

In 1991, a document was signed, as an addition to the Treaty, to give added environmental protection to Antarctica and its surrounding seas.

Called "The Madrid Protocol" because it was signed in that city, it places an indefinite ban on mining or exploration for minerals. It also sets some new rules for the protection of the Antarctic's flora and fauna, managing and disposing of waste, and preventing marine pollution. It created some protected areas and a standard of principles that all who visit and work in Antarctica must follow.

Antarctica is the only continent where all nations have worked together to create agreed environmental standards. No one nation or person can own Antarctica — but we are all responsible for it.

The flags show the nations that meet regularly to discuss the Treaty. They are called the "Consultative Parties." These nations include the original 12 (indicated by an asterix*) that signed the Treaty and other nations that have large research programs in Antarctica. As of 2005, there are also a further 18 nations that are part of the Treaty. These nations are called the "Acceding States."

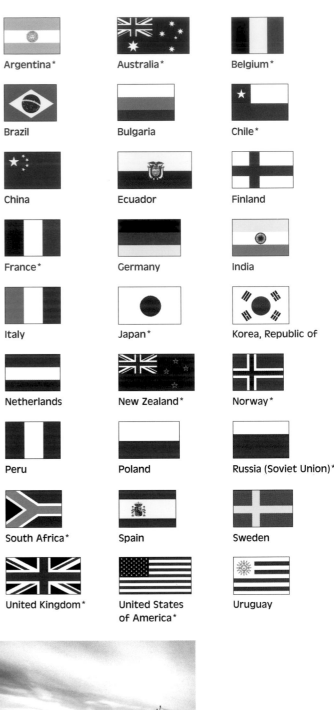

Argentina*	Australia*	Belgium*
Brazil	Bulgaria	Chile*
China	Ecuador	Finland
France*	Germany	India
Italy	Japan*	Korea, Republic of
Netherlands	New Zealand*	Norway*
Peru	Poland	Russia (Soviet Union)*
South Africa*	Spain	Sweden
United Kingdom*	United States of America*	Uruguay

Flags of various nations flutter at the Ceremonial South Pole.

Scientists from around the world come to work together in Antarctica.

Mawson ice scape.

INTERNATIONAL CO-OPERATION

As written in the Antarctic Treaty, plans for scientific programs, observations and results should be exchanged and made freely available between countries working in Antarctica. This also means that scientists need to work together on each other's stations, or in the field, in order to achieve their common goals. Antarctica has become a true international family, with different countries working together and helping each other.

This means helping not only with science, but also in emergencies, when resupplying expeditions and for social visits. Some stations have invited each other for Christmas dinner and will help out with necessary equipment and supplies.

Many organizations around the world have been formed to collect and exchange information on Antarctica. Some also co-ordinate scientific research between governments and industry.

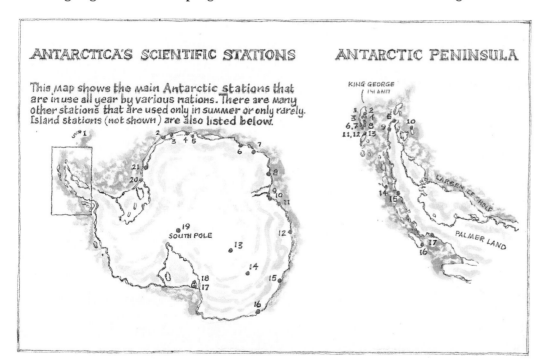

ANTARCTICA'S SCIENTIFIC STATIONS

1. Orcadas (Argentina) 2. Neumayer (Germany) 3. SANAE (South Africa) 4. Maitri (India)
5. Novolazarevskaya (Russia) 6. Syowa (Japan) 7. Molodezhnaya (Russia) 8. Mawson (Australia)
9. Zhongshan (China) 10. Progress (Russia) 11. Davis (Australia) 12. Mirny (Russia) 13. Vostok (Russia)
14. Concordia (France and Italy) 15. Casey (Australia) 16. Dumont D'Urville (France) 17. McMurdo (USA)
18. Scott Base (NZ) 19. Amundsen-Scott (USA) 20. General Belgrano II (Argentina) 21. Halley (UK)

ANTARCTIC PENINSULA STATIONS

1. Commandante Ferraz (Brazil)
2. Henryk Arctowski (Poland)
3. Artigas (Uruguay)
4. Teniente Jubany (Argentina)
5. Esperanza (Argentina)
6. Bellingshausen (Russia)
7. Great Wall (China)
8. King Sejong (Korea)
9. General Bernado O'Higgins (Chile)
10. Vice Comodoro Marambio (Argentina)
11. Presidente Eduardo Frei (Chile)
12. Escudero (Chile)
13. Capitán Arturo Prat (Chile)
14. Palmer (USA)
15. Academician Vernadsky (Ukraine)
16. Rothera (UK)
17. General San Martin (Argentina)

ISLAND STATIONS

Macquarie Island (Australia),
Martin-de-Viviès Ile Amsterdam (France),
Port Aux Francais Iles Kerguelen (France),
Alfred Faure Iles Crozet (France),
Marion Island of Prince Edward Islands (South Africa),
Gough Island (South Africa and Germany),
Bird Island South Georgia (UK),
King Edward Point South Georgia (UK)

UNDERSTANDING ANTARCTICA

MODERN SCIENCE

Modern scientific research in Antarctica began after the signing of the Antarctic Treaty in 1959 (see pages 26–27). Since then, although many of the sciences studied in Antarctica have not changed, the methods and the technology used have altered considerably. As we have gathered knowledge, our understanding of our Earth and our universe has also changed. Science has developed with these advances and also has recognized how important Antarctica and its Southern Ocean are to our world.

Communications dome

Drilling on the ice

Satellites have given us a total picture of the Antarctic continent from space, where we can view the ice sheet, the changing ocean and the weather. At stations and in the field, equipment, laboratories and accommodation have improved and incorporated the latest technologies. Communications are now very sophisticated and connect people through global computer networks. All of these things allow people to be able to work and live in Antarctica for longer periods, but to still have direct communication with the rest of the world.

The satellite-based Global Positioning System provides instant recognition of a scientist's position on the ocean or on land. Some instruments have even been developed to help scientists gather data without being on location, whether in the ocean or on land, and modern laboratories mean scientists can work on their samples or findings before leaving the continent.

Even with these advances, conditions remain very harsh for scientists collecting information in Antarctica. They must often wait to work when the weather allows, whether it's day or night!

Although some things have changed for scientists in the Antarctic, the drive and desire to find out further information has not.

SCIENCE IN ANTARCTICA

Many scientists come to work in Antarctica and the main areas or programs they work under are listed below. Although some scientists stay in Antarctica for the winter, most scientific research is undertaken during the summer months, when stations become full of activity.

Astronomy: The study of the processes by which stars and planetary systems form from dust clouds, and the life and history of the galaxy and the universe.

Aurora

Atmospheric balloons

Atmospheric Sciences: The study and search for any evidence of global climate change, by collecting information on long-term trends in temperature, winds and the density of the upper atmosphere. This includes gathering information for understanding and predicting "space weather."

Biology: The study of a wide range of both terrestrial (earth-dwelling) and marine (ocean, water-dwelling) animals and plants. Biological science looks at their habitats, survival and conservation and the role animals and plants play in the global cycles of biology, geology and chemistry.

Studying seal populations

Collecting data on plant life

Antarctic Marine Living Resources: This program is designed to provide information through research about the best management plans to achieve ecological sustainability of fisheries in the Southern Ocean.

Cosmic Ray Physics: The collection of information about the effect of the Sun's magnetic field and solar wind or flares on the radiation near the Earth. Scientists measure the radiation in near-earth space and the effects this has on space weather.

Geosciences: The study of the processes that have formed and shaped Antarctica and the surrounding ocean. Understanding these processes can provide a history of Antarctica's geological, geophysical and climatic past from which predictions for the future can be made. Of importance is the influence of glacial events on the Earth's climate.

Glaciology: The study of the history of the Earth as found in sediments, dust and gases such as carbon dioxide and oxygen that are trapped within the ice. Glaciologists examine the effects of the Antarctic ice sheet and sea ice cover on water transport, ocean currents and climate predictions, both past and present.

In the laboratory

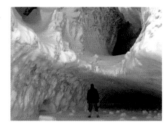

In the field

Human Biology and Medicine: The study of the changes that happen to humans in Antarctica. It looks at how human efficiency can be improved and how these improvements and studies can help to plan activities in other extreme environments, such as deep space.

Human Impacts: The study of the ways in which humans have had an impact in Antarctica. A Human Impacts Researcher investigates how future impact can be kept to a minimum and how past environmental damage can be cleaned up.

Science under the ice

Monitoring instruments

Oceanography: Oceanographers study the ever-changing Southern Ocean and its ecosystem. They study its role and importance to the health of the world's oceans and what effects its movement and distribution have on global oceanic circulation and on the world's climate.

FUTURE SCIENCE

The future of science in Antarctica will be exciting and as much of a challenge as the present! As we understand more about Antarctica and its vital role in the Earth's environment we are building up large stores of knowledge, called databases. Using these databases we are able to create a history of the past, from which we can determine what has changed and how. This enables us to better understand how everything is interconnected. Any change to one part of Antarctica and its surrounding ocean will bring about an effect on one or more of the other parts, as well as further afield.

New technology will allow us to see further than we have seen before. Satellites will provide us with constant and precise measurements of whether the ice sheet is increasing or decreasing. We will be able to track the paths of icebergs that break off the tongues of glaciers and monitor the health of the Southern Ocean. Miniature instruments will be carried by some seals and penguins. The information gathered will reveal secrets about their lives, how they move through their environment, what they feed on and what they need to survive. Then satellites, high in the sky above Antarctica, will relay this information to laboratories around the world.

There will be much more 'big' science, using very high-tech and very expensive equipment, such as torpedoes that can move under the ice collecting information and submarines that will take people down to more than 4 miles below the ocean's surface.

In the future, scientists will treat Antarctica far more gently than before. All wastes will be removed and our reliance on oil for electricity generation will be reduced through the use of wind power. We will also find ways to clear up the mess made long ago.

The common bond created through the nations working in Antarctica will continue. Working together and sharing the valuable research and information gathered, there is great hope that the future will bring a continued respect for and desire to protect this most important continent.

Professor Michael Stoddart
Chief Scientist
Australian Antarctic Program
Australian Antarctic Division

MAPPING THE ENVIRONMENT

The environment includes everything that surrounds us. It is the land, the ocean, our atmosphere and deep space. Collecting information, or data, about our environment is important for us to understand our world and our universe and note any changes that occur.

Information is gathered in many ways – photographs taken from helicopters and satellites, signals sent from deep space, laser light detection, tide gauges, sonar and ice cores are just a few. This information is made available in a variety of formats. Maps and graphs, online images and recorded sound all help us build varied pictures of the Antarctic environment.

Collage of aerial photographs with topographical map overlay. Béchervaise Island.

LISTENING TO OUR UNIVERSE

Antarctica offers the best conditions in the world for studying our atmosphere and space. It is dry, cold, clear of dust and virtually empty of artificial lighting and noise. Astronomers can study the processes of the universe, how stars and planetary systems are formed, without great interference.

Surface and underground observatories collect information on cosmic rays. These are high-energy charged particles that travel through space. They are affected by the magnetised regions of the solar system that they pass through. Normally harmless, they can create havoc as they reach Earth by interfering with satellites, electronics and even ground-based power systems.

The Sun not only emits radiation in the form of light and heat, but also emits a stream of protons and electrons known as the solar wind. This gusty solar wind flows at an average speed of 265 miles per second and even faster when the Sun erupts, producing solar flares. The solar wind particles collide with the Earth's magnetic field. Some particles then flow down the magnetic field lines

Notes from an atmospheric and space physicist
Physics: *The study of the make up (properties) and interactions of matter and energy.*

Dr. Ray Morris:
"I have wintered three times in Antarctica working as an upper atmosphere physicist. My research was looking at the interaction of particles from the solar wind with the Earth's magnetic field. This work has gained me some awards.

"On my first trip to Antarctica I was inspired by the awesome visual display of the 'aurora australis'. I was also captivated by the majesty of Antarctica itself and its wildlife.

"I am now a senior scientist and was Program Manager of the Atmospheric and Space Physics group at the Australian Antarctic Division for the past ten years. Our group studies global climate change in the Earth's polar atmosphere, and watches for the impact of space weather in the Antarctic upper atmosphere.

"The Antarctic experience involves a mix of really interesting people, who come from all sorts of lives to live and work together. Speaking on behalf of the expeditioner scientists I work with, we think we're the luckiest people around. We are able to combine our scientific work with the Antarctic wilderness and then travel the world to let others know what we have found."

A magnificent aurora illuminates the night sky.

surrounding the Earth toward the northern and southern polar regions.

These charged particles impart energy to atoms and molecules in the upper polar atmosphere above 62 miles. A spectacular colorful light show or "aurora australis" illuminates the southern sky as excess energy is released from the energized atoms and molecules in the form of light.

The intense colors (red, green and blue) and the movement of the aurora are the focus of scientific study on processes in the upper atmosphere. This is a chaotic realm, changeable as the weather, windier than any mountain peak and as electric as a city night.

The aurora is the visible sign of space weather processes. The ability to forecast space weather will have important benefits for technology. Physicists in Antarctica use radar, optical, magnetometers and other instruments to study the effects of space weather.

POTENTIAL PROBLEMS
GLOBAL WARMING

The Earth has a natural greenhouse effect, for without it the Earth would be extremely cold. Ice cores and the ocean can give us information regarding the different gases in our atmosphere, including greenhouse gases, which help absorb and trap the heat released from the land and ocean. One of these gases is carbon dioxide. Humans have created more carbon dioxide than our Earth's natural systems may be able to recycle. Carbon is stored in fossil fuels and forests. The burning of these fuels and the clearing and burning of forests releases carbon, which combines with oxygen to make carbon dioxide. Oceans absorb carbon dioxide from the atmosphere. The Southern Ocean's deep water currents are essential in trapping carbon dioxide, sending it to the bottom of the ocean. Scientific research in Antarctica is helping us to understand the effects that increases in greenhouses gases have on the Earth's environment and their role in global warming.

A HOLE IN THE OZONE LAYER

The Earth's atmosphere is made up of many layers. One of these layers is called the ozone layer and it absorbs a large amount of the Sun's harmful ultraviolet radiation. In the 1980s scientists working in Antarctica observed that ozone levels above Antarctica were being depleted. It is known that the chlorine in CFCs (chlorofluorocarbons) once used in aerosol sprays and refrigerators has made its way into the polar atmosphere. In winter, the chlorine attaches to particles of ice in the cold polar atmosphere. In spring, when sunlight returns to Antarctica, the ice particles melt and chemical reactions between ozone and chlorine follow. This process results in a loss of ozone, and the thinning of the ozone layer. By reducing the release of these harmful chemicals, with time the ozone layer may recover.

The coldest region of the Earth's environment is the layer above the ozone layer, the "mesopause region." Temperatures here can be $-184\,°F$ in the polar regions in summer. There is an increase in ice crystals forming and creating brilliant night luminous clouds or "noctilucent clouds" in polar regions. Physicists are using radar and optical instruments to monitor the weather systems in this layer to find out if the changes are from natural causes or from increases in greenhouse gases.

UNDERSTANDING OURSELVES

As Antarctica is so isolated, the physical and mental health of the people who work there is of great importance. The polar medical doctor is an essential part of any team in Antarctica.

Apart from watching and monitoring the health and concerns of expeditioners they must also be nurse and cleaner, surgeon and dentist. Many doctors are also involved in medical research. Living in an extreme environment like Antarctica can compare to living in space, where people are both isolated and living in a confined area. Some research may help not only people working in the polar regions, but the future explorers of space.

During the winter months, a doctor working in Antarctica must be prepared for anything, as in most cases leaving the continent is impossible. They rely on medical staff away from Antarctica to be their support when needed. Communicating by satellite and computers, laboratory results, X-rays and other information can be sent from polar doctors back to their support staff. Some expeditioners undergo training before coming to Antarctica to be able to assist the doctor if an operation is necessary.

 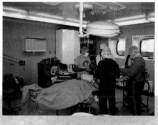

Notes from a polar doctor

Dr. Madeleine Wilcock, AAM*:
"To have been a doctor in Antarctica was an enormous privilege and challenged me both personally and professionally. I was the only woman in a wintering expedition of 21 people at Mawson station. That in itself was an extraordinary experience!

"I was very aware of our remoteness and the need for us to be able to cope with any accident or emergency. I became a "jack-of-all-trades" as I performed dentistry, physiotherapy, X-rays, blood tests and surgery during the year. I was also involved in gathering data for NASA (National Aeronautics and Space Administration) in the United States. Our psychological response to being some of the most isolated people on Earth will be used as a model for human behavior in space.

"I was fortunate to be able to visit many beautiful places in Antarctica. I was awestruck by the majestic emperor penguins, towering jade icebergs and the relentless howling winds. I particularly enjoyed being part of a team and being able to make a contribution as a woman and a doctor."

*Australia Antarctic Medal

SUPPORTING SCIENCE

Undertaking science in Antarctica would be impossible without the large groups of people who support the scientists in their work. At home and on the continent there are many things to organize to keep these isolated stations in operation—from ordering and cooking the food, to purchasing building materials, keeping the power going and much more. Most stations in Antarctica conduct some science during the winter months, but the majority of people arrive for the spring and summer.

Summer: changeover of winter and summer expeditioners at Mawson station.

Winter: wintering expeditioners at Mawson station.

WORKING TOGETHER

All people who live and work in Antarctica take on other work responsibilities apart from their own professions. Everyone must be a cleaner, taking care of their own equipment, helping others and working around the station. Everyone gets their turn to cook and clean up and help with everyday chores. At times of resupply, all hands are needed to help bring in and store supplies and equipment.

Apart from their own daily work schedules, some people take on added responsibilities such as being postmaster, fire officers or storepersons.

PROFESSIONS IN ANTARCTICA

Although in summer the number of people at each station swells, the basic wintering team at a station will consist of:

Station leader
Medical doctor
Meteorological technical officer
Meteorological observer
Plant inspector (senior diesel mechanic)
Mechanic
Electrician
Plumber
Carpenter
Communications officer
Chef
Wintering scientists

In summer, as added work is undertaken in preparation for the next winter, engineers, computer scientists, maintenance and building teams can arrive. Helicopter pilots and engineers are needed. Extra staff arrive to observe and work in fields from occupational health and safety to field training.

Building and maintenance teams undertake essential work at Antarctic stations.

Loading supplies. Supplies often need to be transported between stations and field camps. Here, a quad is being loaded onto a light aircraft.

The maintenance and observation of equipment is necessary for an Antarctic station to function. Here, an electrician checks equipment.

Everyone takes a turn helping out in the station's kitchen. Here, a helper (called a "slushy") works with the station's chef to prepare a meal.

Helicopters and barges are used at some stations to unload supplies from ship to shore.

A helicopter lifts building materials from the deck of the *Aurora Australis*, bound for Macquarie Island.

Notes from an electrician and fire officer

Paul Gleeson:

"My job in Antarctica is as an electrician, but it is not just putting in lots of wire and light bulbs. Electricians are responsible for the placement and maintenance of some very special equipment.

"At some stations, we have a computerized system that can tell us exactly what is happening to our buildings. We can use remote control to change some of the buildings' functions, like the inside temperature. This equipment can tell us when there is a problem, like finding a frozen pipe before it bursts. We can also use it to help scientists to monitor their experiments.

"In Antarctica we must be energy efficient and environmentally responsible and a system like this helps us to reduce our fuel usage.

"Sometimes, I also act as a deputy fire officer. As things cannot be replaced or rebuilt easily in Antarctica, one of the biggest dangers we could face is fire. Buildings are kept separate from each other because of the danger of this. Everyone in Antarctica does fire training and we even have our own fire truck.

"I have been to Antarctica five times. It is a beautiful and special place. There is always something new to see and experience."

GETTING THERE

There are two ways to get to Antarctica: by ship or plane. Although some supplies and scientists are flown to Antarctica, the majority of countries still use ships to carry all the supplies that are necessary to survive there. Barrels of fuel, helicopters and trucks jostle for space with reams of toilet paper, building and scientific supplies and boxes of biscuits.

For most countries, the journey to Antarctica by ship is a long one. But most ships make the most of the journey by taking part in scientific surveys of the ocean and sea ice. They have working laboratories on board and play an important role in the observation of animal life and weather patterns of the Southern Ocean.

A journey to Antarctica by plane allows for a quick visit to the continent. Scientists can fly in, do their work and fly out without the long time delays that come with an ocean voyage. Supplies and scientific equipment can also arrive and depart the continent quickly.

Expeditioners greet the arrival and departure of all visiting ships.

BRINGING IT HOME

When people go to Antarctica to work they leave behind their family and friends. Coming home is a wonderful time for everyone. For some, their work continues upon reaching home and for others their work is finished. But for all, they are excited to be reunited with their family and friends and to enjoy the things they have not had for so long. Often, however, there also is sadness at leaving the special family they have created together and many expeditioners return time and again to their Antarctic community.

"The first thing I'm going to do is to roll around in the grass."
Expeditioner, on coming home

SOCIETY ON ICE

> "I remember the day the last ship of summer sailed away from Davis station, weaving slowly through the icebergs as I watched from a lookout. There would be no ship for eight months, no chance to go home. I felt a mix of emotions, sadness, fear and elation all at once, all lodged as a large lump in my throat."
> Rob Easther, Station Leader

ISOLATION

All people who go to work in Antarctica are commonly called "expeditioners." An expeditioner is a person who is involved in a journey or a voyage for a purpose.

When the last ship and plane have left Antarctica, the people left behind, both scientists and support staff, will live in one of the most isolated communities on Earth. Coming from different backgrounds, with different professions and interests, these people will need to rely on each other for friendship, help and for work.

Like in any society, some people will become great friends and others will not get along so well. Whatever differences there may be, the common bond of Antarctica brings these people together. They may miss many things from their normal lives, but they are also aware of the privilege of working in such an environment. This small group of people can become very close.

They all help to maintain the special community they find themselves in. Many take great interest in each other's work and learn new skills, such as carpentry and photography.

Alone on the ice.

MASCOTS

As the expeditioners must bring everything with them that they may need, they often carry little parts of their normal lives with them, or something that reminds them of home. People bring books, games and hobbies, perhaps a special pillow, a musical instrument or a much-loved old sweater. Most people bring something special with them and often this is something that can be shared with others.

Some carry a mascot or toy with them on expeditions. Some of these mascots have found themselves diving to the ocean's depths; others have lived in huts on the ice. Some have been kidnapped between stations and have ended up on many Antarctic journeys.

Often a mascot is created at stations. Some, such as snowmen and ice sculptures, stay for a short time; others are made to stay for years and greet each new expedition that arrives.

Snowman greeting the day on Marion Island.

Mail destined for Antarctic stations.

BRINGING IN THE MAIL

With modern communications, expeditioners in Antarctica can contact their families, friends and fellow workers, wherever they may be. Telephones and computer links through satellites allow instant contact throughout the world. But for most expeditioners, there is nothing like the very personal touch that getting a letter or a parcel from home can bring.

Expeditioners eagerly await the incoming ship or plane that will bring a message from family or friends. The mail is treated with great respect and is the first thing that is unloaded, usually along with some fresh fruit, and given to the expeditioners.

Likewise, a visiting ship or plane can take a personal message or gift from an expeditioner, in the return mail home. Some expeditioners take materials with them so that they can make something special ("Made in Antarctica") and send it home.

ANTARCTIC LANGUAGE

As the countries who have a presence in Antarctica reflect the varying nations of our world, so do their languages. But to communicate with each other a special type of language has evolved. Many words for weather conditions, covering sea ice, snow and land ice, are known and commonly used by all countries.

A specialized Antarctic language has been made up by expeditioners over time. Some examples are:

On the ice: to be in Antarctica

Off the ice: to be anywhere else on Earth (also known as "the real world")

Toast: the mental state induced by long periods on the ice. Symptoms are a prolonged unblinking stare, nervous giggle, etc. (usage: "I'm toast," "You're toast," "We are all toast;" well done, crispy, burnt and charcoal are varying degrees of toast.)

Snotsicles: two long icicles suspended from one's moustache, directly beneath the nostrils; these can grow 1/2 inch or so in a few hours

Snow school: a survival school that teaches expeditioners how to build igloos, etc.

Yellow snow: urinating on the ice creates yellow snow

(You'll find many more of these terms in *The Antarctic Dictionary* by Bernadette Hince, CSIRO Publishing.)

STAMPS

Because Antarctica is a continent it has its own official stamps. Some countries produce postage stamps to commemorate Antarctic events, but all produce stamps of their stations so that when mail is sent back by ship or plane it bears the mark of where it has come from. There are also other more personal stamps that identify areas, and people make up their own stickers and posters.

Selection of stamps from Australian Antarctic and subantarctic stations.

HUMAN IMPACTS

Antarctica is the most pristine continent on Earth, but human activity has had a direct impact on the environment.

From the earliest times when wildlife was exploited through sealing and whaling, humans used Antarctica for their own purposes without any consideration for the environment. Some ships still lie forgotten and rotting in harbors of subantarctic islands. Stations were built and then abandoned. Polluting oils, chemicals and equipment were just left behind.

Scientific research into the human impacts on Antarctica deals with many issues. One is the cleaning and removal of waste from contaminated sites. It also deals with the introduction of foreign plants, animals and materials that are brought to and could harm Antarctica. It's also concerned with working towards alternative energy systems for use on the continent, and looks at the disruption that any human presence has on the flora, fauna and physical structure of the continent.

Study into human impacts helps develop new guidelines for the way in which we can visit and work in Antarctica with as little disruption as possible.

An Adélie penguin amongst empty fuel barrels

Notes from the human impacts research program leader

Dr. Martin Riddle:
"I was offered my first trip to Antarctica by a visiting American scientist who had pioneered the use of scuba (self-contained underwater breathing apparatus) to study Antarctic marine communities. I joined a research team on a trip to McMurdo Station in the Ross Sea. It was probably the most important few months of my life. People either love the Antarctic and are hooked for life — or they don't. I was hooked.

"I am now working in Human Impacts Research and investigating how people in the Antarctic can cause environmental problems. Through scientific research we gain a better understanding of problems and can develop ways in which to reduce our impacts and provide greater environmental protection to Antarctica and its unique flora and fauna. What a privilege it is to work in that wonderful environment, to be doing something so important and, not only that, but to still be able to play around in boats and go diving."

STATIONS AS COMMUNITIES

INSIDE STATIONS

Most countries have tried to make their stations as comfortable as they can for their expeditioners. Apart from working areas and buildings set aside for this, the main living quarters of a station are the center of activity. Most buildings are the reverse of a fridge, with everything cold on the outside.

They usually contain a "cold porch," a place where you can take off the layers of clothing and boots needed for being outside and then enter the heated building. They have a central 'mess' or kitchen and eating area, which also becomes a focus for meetings and social events. Most have entertainment areas where people can meet and play games, watch movies, listen to music and visit the library. There are group communications areas, telephones, doctor's offices, laundry and of course the rooms where expeditioners sleep.

Chef preparing meals at Mawson station.

Looking out from the cosy interior of "The Red Shed," Mawson.

SUPPLIES

Imagine a place where you must take everything you will ever need, a place where you cannot use anything from the environment apart from water to survive. This is Antarctica. Every tiny detail must be considered — from building materials, fuel and vehicles to survival equipment, clothing, food and personal items. Below is just an example of some things taken from one resupply voyage.

Food is very important, and the list below shows a few items for supply to one station.

Notes from a station leader

Rob Easther:

"I first wanted to go on an expedition after looking at photographs of Scott's Hut in the Antarctic; the bright faces of young men sitting at long tables over dinner. The tales of the day's adventures bubbled out of the photographs and the paraphernalia of exploration, harnesses, items of clothing and pieces of equipment hung from the rafters of the hut. They looked safe and content, or so I imagined, with the blizzards raging around the cocoon they had constructed for themselves.

"The first time I went on an expedition to the Antarctic, my main fear was how I would cope with a year away from my family and friends. I was starting out on the adventure of a lifetime. It was actually happening and it suddenly occurred to me — what if I couldn't do it?

"Now, after years of working in Antarctica, I have so many memories to recall. Exploring a route across a glacier, being stuck in the ice on a ship, establishing a new summer base, flying above the ice, lakes and between icebergs.

"My time as a Station Leader still registers as the best job I've ever had. The freedom to make each day an adventure, to help people achieve their work and to harness all those skills and experience and to come up with solutions to the myriad problems that filled the year."

plug cords, screws, pipes, nails, timber, stationery, tyres, blinds

Below are some food items supplied to stations —

12 boxes of toothpicks (500 in each box)
180 bottles soy sauce
15 cartons of olive oil
300 packets of Tim Tams
15 cartons of eggs (dipped in oil to keep them fresh) 360 eggs in each carton
15 cartons of chocolate self-saucing pudding
kilograms of chillies
15 × 11 litre tubs of vanilla ice cream
300kg plain flour
15 cartons of blackcurrant cordial
9kg broccoli

mattresses, lamps, cup hooks, radio parts, mops, rubber boats, toilet paper, needles and cotton, saucepans, soap, boot polish, band aids, cutlery, shower roses, telephones, batteries, tents

Mawson station, Australia

Vostok, Russia

Syowa, Japan

McMurdo, USA

LIVING IN THE FREEZER

A typical station kitchen is like the kitchen of a large restaurant. But getting the food from the ship or plane to the station requires different thinking than just taking the groceries from the shop to your house. Lettuces, tomatoes, potatoes and eggs — in fact anything that would freeze and be ruined — must be kept warm until it reaches the station.

Food is very important in Antarctica and rations for people who go out on field expeditions are different than at the station. Freeze dried and canned food along with rice and noodles form the basis of field diets.

Eating at the station is also a time for people to come together.

An Antarctic chef must consider all the dietary requirements of the people at the station, make healthy food and provide a good variety of dishes.

Some stations grow some food by hydroponics. No introduced soils are allowed into Antarctica, so plants are kept in a separate building. Grown in large troughs or pots, they survive in a mixture of chemicals and water and a type of synthetic pebble that their roots can grow into. Fresh vegetables and herbs provide a delight for expeditioners.

Growing hydroponic vegetables and herbs at Mawson station.

Boiling water is thrown into the air and freezes before it reaches the ice.

"You can't just run out to the shop and buy something. Sometimes it's important to ration the chocolate biscuits. You learn to never leave home without your toolbox and recipe book. One morning my main freezer inside the station was −4°F, but outside it was −29°F. Sometimes it was easier to put the week's rations of frozen food just outside the back door of the kitchen."
Michael Lunney, Chef

Notes from an Antarctic chef

Tim Last:

"A chef in Antarctica has a lot of jobs on and away from the station. The chef is responsible for packing and storing and cooking the food that is brought down. Apart from cooking three hot meals a day, a chef often helps scientists prepare food to take with them away from the station. This can be making up rations from one night to three months.

"The chef is the heartbeat of the station, always knowing where everyone is at anytime, so you don't cook too much or too little. The kitchen and dining area is also the social hub of the station, and there are always people to help. We call them 'slushies'.

"There are special occasions, such as festive times like Christmas and birthdays. At the middle of winter, called midwinter, a huge banquet of food is made. Saturday nights are treated as special nights and expeditioners dress up and we sometimes have themes, like Italian nights, etc. My favorite things to cook are desserts and cakes, so I had many opportunities for that.

"In my year, together with the 'slushies', we produced over 37,500 meals. We drank over 145 gallons of juice, ate over 485 pounds of rice, 600 dozen eggs, 3,750 pounds of meat, 750 pounds of frozen vegetables and 110 pounds of cooking chocolate. One of the major jobs of a chef is to make sure that the food will last until the next ship comes in. This can be quite difficult, especially hiding the chocolates from hungry expeditioners.

"I always wanted to go to Antarctica. It has been a long-term dream for me, and I got to do what I like to do—cook."

SURVIVAL IN THE FIELD

Living away from a station is a very different experience again. Sometimes expeditioners camp in tents. At other times they have more permanent structures such as huts called apple, melon or zucchini huts depending on their size and shape.

Some types of accommodation, which look like little buildings, are called traverse vehicles and are towed across the ice. Whatever the accommodation, it must contain equipment for sleeping and survival, food, cooking facilities and radio communication.

In a tent, expeditioners are very aware of the environment and often have the howl of the wind as a constant companion. They use snow to weigh down their tents against the strong wind and sometimes must shovel snow away so they can get out of their tents.

SURVIVAL AND TRAINING

Our presence in Antarctica is not natural. In this landscape of ice and snow, performing everyday duties can be extremely difficult. There are no trees or bushes to make a hasty shelter if needed. Any trip away from a station means that everything expeditioners need to survive must be taken with them.

Wind and wet conditions, even sweat, can chill and sometimes freeze any exposed areas of skin, causing frostnip or frostbite. Chilling of the whole body is called hypothermia, or exposure, and this can be fatal. Expeditioners must dress properly for the conditions and carry spare clothing with them.

"In a tent made between two quads, parked into the wind, I felt I was inside a packet of potato chips, with the continuous crunching and rustling of the tent. Exhausted, as I hadn't slept all night, I was eager to leave the tent as soon as morning came. I looked out and saw the katabatic winds picking up snow and dancing it over an ice cliff, luminous in the morning sunshine. I forgot my tiredness as I became elated by the nature I was privileged to witness and be a part of."
Dr. Barbara Smith, Glaciologist

An extremely cold expeditioner.

A polar pyramid tent.

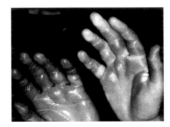

Fingers showing frostbite.

Apple and melon huts in the field.

ANTARCTIC CLOTHING

Layers of warm clothing are important.

neck and head bands

Woollen shirt

thermal underwear

thick socks

warm pants

beanie
Woollen jumper

gloves

windproof pants

ice pick for walking on ice

windproof jacket

balaclava

sheepskin hat and goggles

big mittens (for colder conditions)

freezer suit

boots (and chains on ice)

igloo   Shelters can be made of snow. Hard or compressed snow can be cut into blocks to make an igloo. Holes can be dug into snow drifts to make snow caves.   snow cave

Inside a melon hut. Apple huts can be extended to make larger huts, called melon huts.

All expeditioners attend survival and training courses, since simple problems can easily turn into dangerous situations in Antartica. They learn to work together in a group and to use the buddy system, always watching out for each other and warning others of imminent danger from, say, a crevasse up ahead.

Expeditioners also learn how to use machinery and field equipment, motorized vehicles such as quads and skidoos, and radios and other forms of communication. Everything must be considered, from walking safely on ice, skiing and absailing, to how to build shelter—from tents and huts to igloos and ice caves.

The four main dangers for expeditioners that have led to accidents over the years are blizzards, crevasses, thin sea ice and problems with transport machinery such as quads.

Abseil training in Antarctica, showing a rescue.

TRANSPORT ON THE ICE

Modern forms of transport make travel in Antarctica easier for today's expeditioners. Dogs are not allowed in Antarctica any more, so some expeditioners pull their own sleds. This is called manhauling.

Some trucks, tractors and earth-moving equipment are used in Antarctica, but most of the vehicles are used for travel across the snow and ice. Small rubber boats are used for water transport, and helicopters fly expeditioners and supplies. Some aircraft also are used in Antarctica. All vehicles need special fuel and anti-freeze and carry some emergency rations, equipment, a first-aid kit, and a radio for communication.

Quads are lightweight four-wheel drive cycles fitted with high-flotation tires. They are used around stations and in the field.

Hagglunds are heavy vehicles with rubber tracks. There is a front cab for passengers and a rear cab for equipment. They can also travel on thick sea ice.

A skidoo can travel long distances and can pull sledges with loads up to 2,500 pounds. They have specially designed rubber tracks and skis.

On the continent, clothing has to be windproof, but not waterproof. In the subantarctic, clothing is similar, but needs to be covered by a waterproof layer.

Expeditioners take extra clothing with them when out in the field. They also take along their own toilet. A plastic flour bin and plastic bags are good for solids. Women have a device to urinate through, so there's no need to undress.

Don Reid (Uncle Don)
Clothing Storeman, AAD.*
Uncle Don says, "If you want to look cool in Antarctica, you'll get cold."

plastic tube inside

Tractors can be attached to room-like sleds to form trains that have living and workshop facilities, scientific equipment and other essentials.

Light aircraft are used at some stations to transport expeditioners, equipment and supplies.

*Australian Antarctic Division

39

THE SUBANTARCTIC

The vast Southern Ocean surrounding Antarctica contains many islands. The true subantarctic islands lie close to the Antarctic Polar Front, where the colder Antarctic waters meet with the warmer waters of the north. This is an area of wild, wet and windy weather. While still extremely cold, the temperatures differ from the Antarctic continent and support a great variety of life. As the Antarctic Peninsula winds its way up towards South America, its islands are mostly ice covered and are often locked to land by pack ice. Some islands have ice caps and glaciers, while others further north receive rain and support a variety of plant life. Although they are such tiny dots of land, these islands are extremely important breeding sites for the seals and birds that feed in the Southern Ocean. Plant life has evolved to cope with the extreme conditions and many of the plant species are only found on subantarctic islands.

Some of these islands were born through volcanic activity and have high, mountainous peaks. A few, such as Heard and McDonald Islands, still have active volcanoes. Originally visited by whalers and sealers, many of them now have scientific stations and are wildlife refuges. Studying the plants and animals, the Earth, ocean and varying temperatures gives us essential information about the environment of the Southern Ocean.

There are many species of plants and animals on subantarctic islands. Just some of these are listed below.

Gentoo penguins are slightly smaller than Adélie and chinstrap penguins.

King penguins are the second largest penguins, smaller and lighter than emperor penguins.

Royal penguins look similar to macaroni penguins (the most abundant of the penguins), but are only found on Macquarie Island.

Rockhopper penguins are found on the cold-temperate islands. They make their breeding sites close to the water, so they can quickly hop and swim between the ocean and their nests.

Elephant seals in tussock grass (see also page 18).

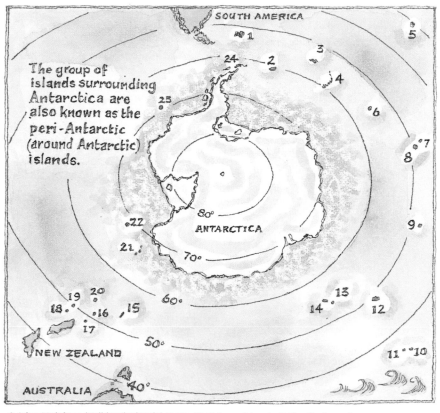

The group of islands surrounding Antarctica are also known as the peri-Antarctic (around Antarctic) islands.

Fur seals were once hunted for their coats, but are now found in large numbers throughout the Southern Ocean's islands.

1. Islas Malvinas (Falkland Islands) 2. South Orkney Islands 3. South Georgia
4. South Sandwich Islands 5. Gough Island 6. Bouvetøya 7. Prince Edward Island 8. Marion Island
9. Iles Crozet 10. Ile Amsterdam 11. Ile St Paul 12. Iles Kerguelen 13. McDonald Islands
14. Heard Island 15. Macquarie Island 16. Auckland Islands 17. The Snares 18. Bounty Islands
19. Antipodes Islands 20. Campbell Island 21. Balleny Islands 22. Scott Island 23. Peter 1 Øy
24. South Shetland Islands

Kelp and ocean

Wandering albatross

Sooty albatross chick

Maquarie island cabbage

Acaena minor

Moss and ice

Pleurophyllum

Kerguelen cabbage

THE NON-EXISTENT ISLANDS

There are written and charted reports of eighteen islands in the Southern Ocean, but their actual existence is not known. They have been recorded in sea charts through time and given names. Some may have been created as a hoax, so that sealers and whalers could keep their hunting grounds secret. Some may be the rotting remnants of large icebergs, or perhaps once existed, but have since sunk through volcanic activity. Whether they actually exist or not, some can still be found on ocean charts. Some of these islands are marked on the map (above).

Ice-bound islands
(e.g. Bouvetøya, South Orkney, South Shetland, South Sandwich, Peter 1 Øy, Scott and Balleny Island)
Some islands close to the continent are always subject to the varying conditions of the Southern Ocean. In winter, they are surrounded by pack ice and in summer the temperature can rise above freezing. Many animals breed on these islands and in ice-free areas there are deep banks of peat moss and some flowering plants.

Antarctic Maritime islands
(e.g. South Georgia, Heard and MacDonald Islands)
South Georgia, Heard and MacDonald Islands are all close to the Antarctic Polar Front and have ice caps and glaciers. They experience wild winds and wet weather. They are free from pack ice and do experience temperatures above freezing. There are coastal grasses, plants and mosses. Many animals breed on these islands in summer.

Cold-temperate islands
(e.g. Kerguelen, Crozet, Macquarie, Marion, Prince Edward, Falklands/Malvinas, Campbell and Auckland Islands)
Many islands are a long way from the influence of the Antarctic continent. They experience warmer temperatures, but are wet and windy. Mostly free of permanent snow, they have grasses, plants and mosses. Many animals come to breed on the island beaches.

THE FUTURE

A RESPONSIBLE FUTURE

With our growing knowledge of the Antarctic environment and its need for protection, we need to place a careful watch on all human activity. Although there are many protections in place, some people will always be interested in exploiting Antarctica's resources.

Some countries still hunt and kill animals, such as whales, in protected waters. Large amounts of krill, fish and squid are taken by fishing boats. Seals and birds are killed when they become tangled in the nets and lines of fishing boats. Antarctica is still under pressure from countries that wish to explore and mine minerals, even though this has been banned.

It is the only place in the world where all nations work together to maintain the environment. Any loss of true internationalism in Antarctica would be an enormous loss for our world. A future for Antarctica is a future in which we all are responsible.

TOURISM

As the stories of Antarctica have returned, our desire to visit this rare and beautiful continent has increased. Its unique wildlife, beauty and wilderness have attracted the business of tourism.

Some tourists fly over Antarctica during the summer months, but most visit in cruise ships. Anyone can go to Antarctica, but because of the very difficult conditions of reaching the continent and surviving there, most people travel and visit in organized groups.

There are strict rules for anyone who visits Antarctica and these cover safety and the protection of the environment and wildlife. But any human presence in Antarctica is unnatural and an increase in the numbers of visitors is a concern and is monitored. Tourism is growing at about 10 percent per year. The challenge for the future is how we can protect the Antarctic environment with an increase in visitor numbers.

Tourists can take nothing away from Antarctica except photographs and memories. But for those fortunate enough to visit, the experience is a journey of a lifetime. The rare qualities of Antarctica create an enormous respect for the continent. Everyone returns with an understanding of the great privilege it is to visit Antarctica.

Antarctica: a child's view

Kate Ledingham:
"My parents are both involved with working in Antarctica, and together we have traveled on four tourist trips to the continent. I have been so lucky to have been able to travel with my family to Antarctica.

"The first time I went I was only five years old. I was the only child on the trip and everyone was really, really nice to me. Everyone would pick me up and give me lots of hugs. The second time I went I was ten years old. I have been on ships from South America to the Antarctic Peninsula, visited the Ross Sea, and the subantarctic islands of South Georgia, Falklands and Macquarie. It's such fun on the ship. I got to use the speaker to announce things like afternoon tea, and helped people in the shop and in the bar and delivered things like our daily newsletter. I made great friends and you meet some really interesting people with the most amazing stories of all the places in the world they have been to.

"The Southern Ocean can be really scary and creepy. I was frightened in the Ross Sea, with waves crashing over our ten-storey high ship. Everywhere you look there are really big waves. From horizon to horizon, these high, rolling waves look as if they can eat you up. But it was so beautiful once we got into the ice. It's quiet; everything is muffled. I felt really calm as if I was in a dream and I was just floating around.

"I remember beautiful scenes like being in a huge fiord when the sun was going down. The ice plummeted straight into a turquoise sea. King penguins coming out to greet our ship looked like they were waving to us and calling out to come and play. I loved the penguins, the mad way they'd slip and slide across the ice. The elephant seals reminded me of bulldozers, climbing and bumping up against each other. And the ice was amazing. It just seemed to go on forever.

"I was so lucky to be able to go and I get so angry now when I see pictures of rubbish that has not been cleared away. I hate the whaling that some countries continue to do and all the birds that get caught in the fishing nets. My trips have given me a great respect for the wildlife and this wonderful clean and pure environment. We have to look after this place.

"Antarctica is so beautiful. I don't really have one special memory of this place. It's the whole thing. It's Antarctica, you know."

Tourism in Antarctica.

WHAT YOU CAN DO

There are many ways you can help protect Antarctica, its oceans and its wildlife. Your voice and your actions can make a difference! Talk with your family and friends about the importance of Antarctica. Ask your teachers to discuss Antarctica and its future with you and your classmates.

By doing your own research, you can find out about the issues that interest you. Antarctica's scientific and human history is very recent compared to the other continents of the world. Information changes and is being gathered continuously, so there is much good current information on Antarctica to be found. The Internet is a major source for the most up-to-date information and images. The following list of sites will help you travel on your own journey to Antarctica.

www.asoc.org
Site for the Antarctic and Southern Ocean Coalition, a global group of environmental NGOs with over 240 members in over 40 states worldwide. ASOC has worked for 25 years to ensure that the Arctic continent, its surrounding islands and the Southern Ocean survive as unspoiled wilderness.

www.aad.gov.au
The Australian Antarctic Division's website. Educational, fun, and packed full of history and current information.

www.aad.gov.au/classroom/textversion/resources_text.htlm
A great information site that includes Web addresses of the Antarctic programs around the world, along with a list of Antarctic education and information sites, as well as virtual tours, picture library databases, interactive explorations, experiments, and live telecasts.

www.antarctica.ac.uk
The British Antarctic Survey (BAS) is a component of the Natural Environment Research Council and for almost 60 years has undertaken Britain's scientific research on and around the Antarctic continent. Provides a good historical overview as well as good current information on key topics.

http://usarc.usgs.gov
The U.S. Antarctic Resource Center (USARC) at the U.S. Geological survey (USGS) maintains the U.S.'s most comprehensive collection of Antarctic maps, charts, satellite images and photos produced by the U.S. and the other member nations of SCAR (Scientific Community of Antarctic Research), which can be found at www.scar.org, and includes up-to-date general statistics about Antarctica as well as abundant scientific information about Antarctica and the role of the Antarctic in the earth system.

Other excellent sites:
www.ccamlr.org The Commission for the Conservation of Antarctic Marine Living Resources;
www.iaato.org The International Association of Antarctica Tour Operators site, with information on environmental tourism and a gorgeous gallery of photos;
http://astro.uchicago.edu/cara/southpole.edu The Center for Astrophysical Research in Antarctica, South Pole Adventure Web page, with hands-on scientific experiments, photos, live Web cams and more;
www.pbs.org/wgbh/nova/shackleton/1914 A good site for learning about Shackleton and his voyage to Antarctica.

ACKNOWLEDGEMENTS

There are so many people who helped with the production of this book, from my mother and father's continued support of my ideas, my husband, Peter, daughter, Tully and step-daughter, Isa, who never tired of the Antarctic maps that still wallpaper our house, the Australian Antarctic Division (AAD) who made my journey possible, all of those who shared the voyage south with me, the fabulous captain and crew of the RSV Aurora Australis, who enriched the experience with their immense capability and humour, my editor for her patience and commitment and my wonderful designer, who now has a little ice in her veins.

I would particularly like to thank the wonderful staff of the Australian Antarctic Division, Antarctic CRC, and the University of Tasmania, who freely gave of their time, experience, knowledge and skills, and with patience and friendship, continuously supported this project.

This book would not have been possible without the generous contributions of the following people:
Kathryn Barker, Nathan Bindoff, Kevin Bell, Dr Dana Bergstrom, Martin Betts, Peter Boyer, Henk Brolsma, Harry Burton, Simon Cash, Neal Costello, John Cox, Dr Andrew Davidson, Jonothan Davis, Rob Easther, Phil Gard, John Gibson, Dr Peter Gormly, Dr Peter Harris, Liz Haywood, Petra Heil, Dr Graham Hosie, Dr John Innis, Lyn Irvine, Dr Kerry Knowles, Rod Ledingham, Dr Hau Ling, Dr Vicki Lytle, Nick Lovibond, Dr Des Lugg, Professor Harvey Marchant, Vin Morgan, Dr Ray Morris, Richard Mulligan, Wayne Papps, Sandra Potter, Dr Tony Press, Professor Pat Quilty, Don Reid, Dr Martin Riddle, Annie Rushton, Ursula Ryan, Dr Barbara Smith, Andie Smithies, Dr Ian Snape, Professor Michael Stoddart, Dr Peter Sullivan, Dr Kerrie Swadling, Dr Jean Syme, Lloyd Symons, Andrew Tabor, Dr Doug Thost, Michael Trotter, Rene Wanless, Robert Warren, Graeme Watt, Dr Dick Williams, Phil Wood, Dr Simon Wright, Anthony Young, from the Australian Antarctic Division, Antarctic CRC and the University of Tasmania. Steve Pendlebury, Bureau of Meteorology, Antarctic Section, Hobart; Esteban de Salas, CCAMLR; Lesley Reece, Fremantle Children's Literature Centre, Perth; Mark Pharaoh, Mawson Antarctic Collection, Adelaide; Paul Livingston, Damian Cole, National Library of Australia, Canberra; Dick Burgess, P&O Polar; Margaret Harman, Tasmanian Library, State Library of Tasmania; Jack Sayers, COMNAP.

For their help, stories and support, (not previously mentioned): Paul Brown, Pat Chamberlain, Dave Clement, Eric Donnay, Murray Doyle, Peter Dunbar (The Ice Pirate), Jean-Claude Duplessy, Phillipa Foster, Paul Gleeson, John Hoelscher, Sandra Hodgson, Rebecca Jeffcoat (The MET Fairy), Kate Kiefer, Patrick Kildea, Tim Last, Kate Ledingham, Michael Lunney, Stuart Newman, Gerry O'Doherty (GOD), Peter Pearson, Sue Pickering, John Van Dam, Dr Madeleine Wilcock.

All care has been taken in this publication to acknowledge all sources of reference. I am very grateful to the following organisations and individuals who supplied and gave their permissions for the usage of diagrams, references and photographs: Australian Antarctic Division, National Library of Australia; Australian Antarctic Data Centre; University of Tasmania; Antarctic CRC; Reader's Digest Australia; McGraw Hill Book Company, America; The Australian Greenhouse Office; CSIRO Publishing; Lucy Martin, Scott Polar Research Institute; University of Cambridge; COMNAP; Professor D. J. Drewry; Mr Robert Headland.

Photographic and diagram credits:
p. 3 Horseshoe Harbour, Mawson, Ozzie Ertok, AAD; p. 4 author, Sandra Hodgson; RSV Aurora Australis, B. Griffiths, AAD; p. 6 map by Abraham Ortelius, Typus Orbis Terrarum, Antwerp, 1570. From the Nan Kivell Collection, National Library of Australia; p. 7 mountain panorama, Wayne Papps; iceberg, Wayne Papps; sea surface elevation survey map, NASA; p. 8 Antarctica, NASA; Gondwana diagram adapted from L. A. Lawver, L. M. Gahagan and I. W. D. Dalziel, Dr D. Thost collection; p. 9 Big Ben, K. W. Gooley AAD; Twelfth Lake, Jeff Boyd, AAD; coal seam, J. Baume, AAD; fossilised fern, R. Oldfield; fossilised molluscs, meteorite section, Professor P. Quilty; reconstructed bones, R. E. Fordyce; p. 10 Mawson Escarpment, Australian Antarctic Data Centre; diagram, from Glaciological and Geophysical Folio, Professor D. J. Drewry; ice cliffs, Michael Lunney; Dr B. Smith, collection; Lambert Glacier, Matt Godbold, AAD; p. 12 ice crystals, R. Irving, AAD; hoarfrost, Vin Morgan; sastrugi, Wayne Papps, AAD; firn, Lloyd Symmons; blue ice, Wayne Papps, AAD; crevasse, Michael Hesse; frozen lake, Professor H. Marchant; ice cliffs, Michael Lunney; glacier, Vin Morgan; moraine, Coral Tulloch; crevassed bergs, Dr Barbara Smith; balls of ice, Ken Sheridan, AAD; ice cliff, Michael Lunney; ice core, Dr B. Smith; ice core section, Vin Morgan; p. 13 icy sunset, Coral Tulloch; Peter Dunbar, Gerry O'Doherty; RSV Aurora Australis, Wayne Papps, AAD; p. 14 wild ocean, Wayne Papps, AAD; ice edge, Michael Lunney; grease ice, Professor H. Marchant; bergy bits, bergs at sunset, floes, Kate Kiefer; pancake ice, Sandra Potter; tabular berg, Vin Morgan; large floes, jade berg, Wayne Papps, AAD; p. 15 sun halo, Wayne Papps, AAD; Steve Pendlebury, collection; p. 16 sea floor, Andrew Tabor; under the ice, Dr M. Riddle; p. 17 Kate Kiefer, Doug Ross; phytoplankton, and in sea ice, bacteria and viruses, diatom, parmales, Professor H. Marchant; snow algae, V. Gibson, AAD; moss, Wayne Papps, AAD; lichen, Kate Kiefer; p. 18 krill, squid, ice fish, Mr D. Williams; Adelie and emperor penguins, leopard and weddell seals, seal pup, Michael Lunney; crabeater seal, William Young, AAD; elephant seal, Dr B. Smith; snow petrel, H. Ling, AAD; skua, Murray Price, AAD; p. 19 humpback, minke and southern right whales, AAD; killer whale, Elliot Porter, AAD; Lyn Irvine, Wayne Papps, AAD; p. 22 illustration adapted from The Antarctic Ocean, McGraw Hill Book Company; map of Cook's voyages, adapted from Antarctica, Reader's Digest; Cook's ship, AAD; p. 23 whaling, AAD; p. 24 science, unloading supplies, Rymill collection, AAD; The Endurance, workshop, kitchen duties, against the blizzard, Frank Hurley, AAD; Terra Nova, Captain Oates, Herbert G. Ponting, AAD; p. 25 kitchen duties, Frank Hurley, AAD; South Magnetic Pole Party, T. W. Edgeworth David, AAD; Captain Scott, Herbert G. Ponting, AAD; Wyatt Earp, AAD; sea plane, huskies, Rymill collection, AAD; p. 26 flags, AAD; Ceremonial South Pole, Dr T. Press, collection, AAD; p. 27 scientists, Dr B. Smith; Mawson ice scape, Wayne Papps, AAD; p. 28 communications dome, drilling, Wayne Papps, AAD; aurora, Alan Nutley, AAD; atmospheric balloons, L. Murray, AAD; studying seals, Diana Calder, AAD; collecting data, Kevin Bell, AAD; p. 29 laboratory, Professor H. Marchant collection; in the field, Michael Lunney; under the ice, Dr Ian Snape; monitoring instruments, Wayne Papps, AAD; Professor M. Stoddart, collection; p. 30 photographic collage, Australian Antarctic Data Centre; Dr R. Morris, collection; aurora, D. Day, AAD; p. 31 Dr M. Wilcock, collection; operation, Dr P. Gormly, AAD; p. 32 summer and winter expeditioners, AAD; building, M. Whittle, AAD; loading supplies, A. Cianchi, AAD; maintenance, Paul Gleeson collection; p. 33 slushy, M. Price, AAD; helicopter and barge, Don Chesman, AAD; helicopter, Sandra Potter; Paul Gleeson, collection; expeditioners, F. Jenkins, AAD; p. 34 ice and figure, David Clement; snowman, mall, Kate Kiefer; p. 35 penguin, Dr M. Riddle, collection; p. 36 Rob Easther, collection; chef, Mawson interior, Wayne Papps, AAD; p. 37 Mawson station, Wayne Papps, AAD; Vostok, McMurdo, Lloyd Symons; Syowa, Professor H. Marchant; hydroponics, Tim Last, Coral Tulloch; freezing water, Michael Lunney; p. 38 expeditioner, Dr D. Thost collection; pyramid tent, Diana Calder, AAD; frostbite, O. Merrill, AAD; apple huts, K. Green, AAD; illustration adapted from ANARE field manual; p. 39 melon hut, AAD; abseiling, Michael Lunney; quad, A. Cianchi, AAD; hagglund, Professor H. Marchant; skidoo, Dr B. Smith; tractors, Vin Morgan; aircraft, Wayne Papps, AAD; Uncle Don, Kate Kiefer; p. 40 gentoo, king and rockhopper penguins, elephant seals, Kate Kiefer; royal penguin, G.W. Johnstone, AAD; fur seal, Christo Baars, AAD; p. 41 sooty chick, Macquarie and Kerguelen Island cabbage, acaena minor, pleurophyllum, cold-temperate island, Kate Kiefer; Albatross, Christo Baars, AAD; kelp, moss, Coral Tulloch; ice-bound island, S. Sprunk, AAD; Antarctic maritime island, H. Burton; illustration adapted from Mr Robert Headland; p. 42 Kate Ledingham, collection; tourism, Martin Betts.

BIBLIOGRAPHY

Many articles, and books were consulted for research in this book. The main ones are listed below:

Amundsen, Roald, *Roald Amundsen: My Life As An Explorer,* William Heinemann Ltd, London, 1927

Antarctica: The Extraordinary History of Man's Conquest of the Frozen Continent, Reader's Digest, Sydney, 1985

Armstrong, T., Roberts, B., Swithinbank, C., *Illustrated Glossary of Snow and Ice,* Scott Polar Research Institute, Cambridge, 1966

Back, June Debenham (ed.), *The Quiet Land: The Antarctic Diaries of Frank Debenham,* Bluntisham Books, Erskine Press, England, 1992

Bowden, Tim, *The Silence Calling,* Allen & Unwin, Sydney, 1997

Boyer, Peter, & Kolenberg, Hendrik, *Antarctic Journey: Three Artists in Antarctica,* Australian Government Publishing Service, Canberra, 1988

Cherry-Garrard, Apsley, *The Worst Journey in the World: Antarctic 1910-1913,* Chatto & Windus, London, 1965

Cook, James, *A Voyage Towards the South Pole, and Round the World,* W. Strahan & T. Cadell, London, 1777

Cool Science; Looking South; The Backpackers' Guide to ANARE Science; ANARE Field Manual; ANARE First Aid Manual, Australian Antarctic Division Publications, Kingston, 2000

Davis, John King, *With the "Aurora" in the Antarctic 1911-1914,* Andrew Melrose Ltd, London, 1919

Drewry, D.J. (ed.), *Glaciological & Geophysical Folio,* Scott Polar Research Institute, University of Cambridge, England, 1983

Fothergill, Alastair, *Life in the Freezer: A Natural History of the Antarctic,* BBC Books, London, 1993

Gascoigne, Toss, & Collett, Peter, *Antarctica: Discovery & Exploration,* Curriculum Development Centre, Canberra, 1987

Hince, Bernadette, *The Antarctic Dictionary: A Complete Guide to Antarctic English,* CSIRO Publishing, Collingwood, Australia, and Museum of Victoria, 2000

Hunter Christie, E.W., *The Antarctic Problem,* George Allen & Unwin Ltd, London, 1951

Hurley, Captain Frank, *Argonauts of the South,* G.P. Putnam & Sons, New York & London, 1925

Jacka, Fred, & Jacka, Eleanor (eds), *Mawson's Antarctic Diaries,* Allen & Unwin, Sydney, 1989

Law, Phillip, & Bechervaise, John, *ANARE: Australia's Antarctic Outposts,* Oxford University Press, Melbourne, 1957

Laws, Richard, *Antarctica: The Last Frontier,* Boxtree Ltd, London, 1989

Ley, Willy, *The Poles,* Life Nature Library, Time-Life International, Nederland, 1963

Mawson, Sir Douglas, *The Home of the Blizzard,* Wakefield Press, Adelaide, 1996 (first published, 1930)

May, John, *The Greenpeace Book of Antarctica: A New View of the Seventh Continent,* Dorling Kindersley Ltd, London, 1988

McGonigal, David, & Woodworth, Dr Lynn, *The Complete Story: Antarctica,* The Five Mile Press & Global Book Publishing, Australia, 2001

Medlin, L.K., & Priddle, J., (eds), *Polar Marine Diatoms,* British Antarctic Survey, Cambridge, 1990

Miller, Francis Trevelyan, *The World's Great Adventure: 1000 Years of Polar Exploration,* The John C. Winston Company, Philadelphia, USA, 1930

Monteath, Colin, *Antarctica: Beyond the Southern Ocean,* Harper Collins Publishers, Sydney, 1996

National Aeronautics and Space Administration, *Arctic and Antarctic Sea Ice, 1978-1987: Satellite Passive-Microwave Observations and Analysis,* Washington, USA, 1992

National Geographic Destinations: ANTARCTICA The Last Continent, National Geographic Society, Washington D.C., USA, 1998

British Antarctic Terra Nova Expedition, 1910, Natural History Reports, British Museum of Natural History, London, vols 1-8, 1924-1930

Ommanney, F.D., *South Latitude,* Readers Union Limited, Longmans, Green & Co, London, 1940

Owen, Russell, *The Antarctic Ocean,* McGraw Hill Book Company, Inc, New York, 1941

Ponting, Herbert G., *The Great White South,* Gerald Duckworth, London, 1921

Rubin, Jeff, *Antarctica: A Lonely Planet Travel Survival Kit,* Lonely Planet Publications, Oakland, USA, 1996

Scholes, Arthur, *Seventh Continent,* Allen & Unwin, London, 1953

Scott, Captain Robert F., *Scott's Voyage of the 'Discovery',* John Murray, London, 1929

A Functional Glossary of Ice Terminology, U.S. Navy Hydrographic Office, Washington, USA, 1952

Walton, D.W.H., (ed.), *Antarctic Science,* Cambridge University Press, Cambridge, 1987

Worsley, Frank, *Endurance: An Epic of Polar Adventure,* Geoffrey Bles, London, 1931

GLOSSARY

antifreeze: a substance added to the fluid in radiators that lowers the freezing point of the fluid to prevent engines from freezing.

calve: when a mass of ice breaks off or away from an ice shelf or glacier.

ecology: a branch of biology that focuses on the relationship between organisms (especially plants and animals) and their environment.

ecosystem: living and non-living elements of an environment that interact with each other and so work together as a system.

equinox: the two times of the year in spring and autumn when the Sun crosses the equator and day and night are of equal length everywhere on Earth.

expedition: a journey or voyage made for a particular purpose, such as exploration.

frostbite: a serious medical condition where the skin and underlying tissues become frozen and numb due to long exposure to frigid air or icy winds, often affecting the hands, feet and face.

glacier: a slow-moving river or mass of ice, formed by the accumulation of compressed snow to ice over the years. Under gravity, glaciers move outwards and downwards from higher ground.

greenhouse effect: specific gases in our atmosphere (e.g. carbon dioxide, methane, nitrous oxide, water vapor) that convert light from the sun to heat energy. Like sunlight trapped in a greenhouse, this causes a rise in the Earth's temperature. Most of the heat is re-radiated back from Earth towards space, but some is trapped by these greenhouse gases. This is a natural effect, which keeps the Earth's temperature at a level necessary to support life.

habitat: a place where an animal or plant lives or develops, e.g. a whale in the ocean.

human impacts: the effect of human habitation and presence upon the Antarctic environment.

ice sheet: a large expanse of ice mainly covering areas of land. In Antarctica, the ice that covers the continental land mass is called the ice sheet.

migrate/migration: the periodic travel of animals, such as birds, whales and fish, from one region to another for purposes of survival and reproduction.

Antarctic Polar Front: a front in the Southern Ocean where the cold Antarctic waters and air meet with the warmer northerly waters and air masses.

predator: an animal that preys on other animals for food.

radiation: emission of energy (e.g. from the sun) in the form of rays or waves.

solstice: the two times of the year in summer and winter when the Sun is at its furthest distance from the equator. The Sun is at its lowest path in the sky and the day is the shortest on the winter solstice, while the Sun is at its highest path in the sky and the day is the longest on the summer solstice.

South Magnetic Pole: is the southern point on the Earth's surface where the lines of force from the Earth's magnetic field come together. The position of this pole is not fixed and shifts the distance of approximately 3 miles per year, due to variations in the Earth's magnetic field.

subantarctic: the area around Antarctica (also referred to as the peri-antarctic), comprising the Southern Ocean, the southern waters of the Indian, Pacific and Atlantic Oceans and the remote islands located there.

white-out: a weather condition over snow or ice-covered land caused by cloud that covers the sun. The horizon cannot be seen, as land and sky merge into one and there are no shadows to differentiate objects or distances.

INDEX

SOUTH

50° 40° 30° 20° 10°

60°

50°

• ORCADAS
Islas Malvinas
(Falkland Islands)   South Orkney
                          Islands

NEUMAYER

ô Elephant Island

South
Shetland
Islands   ANTARCTIC PENINSULA

ARGENTINA   HALLEY

70°
      • USHUAIA   LARSEN ICE SHELF   WEDDELL   COATS
        • PUNTA   SEA   LAND
CHILE   ARENAS   GRAHAM LAND   GENERAL •
                                                 BELGRANO II
SOUTH   PALMER LAND   FILCHNER
AMERICA   ICE
                                                    Berkner Island SHELF
80°   FOR   976M
             PENINSULA   RONNE
             STATIONS   ICE SHELF
             SEE MAP
             PAGE 27
                        Alexander Island   • 224M

                                        BELLINGSHAUSEN
                                        SEA   Vinson
                                                       Massif
                                         VENABLE   4897M •   ELLSWORTH MOUNTAINS
                                         ICE SHELF   80°   WEST
50° 90°   ELLSWORTH   2123M
                                Peter I Øy   LAND
                                                 752M HOLLICK-KENYON   ANTARCTICA
                                                       PLATEAU
                                Thurston   714M
                                Island   60°   • 1188M   • 615M
                                70°   MARIE   ROCKEFELLER
                                                                               PLATEAU
                                        AMUNDSEN   BYRD   1550M
                                        SEA
                                                   LAND
                                                   4181M   EDWARD
                                                                       VII
                                                                       LAND
                                                   GETZ
100°   ICE SHELF
                                                                       SULZBERGER
                                                                       ICE SHELF   ROSS
                                                                                        SEA
110°

The Antarctic Circle

Is the southern parallel of latitude
where most of the continent of
Antarctica is to be found. Over
this line, the sun does not set
during midsummer.

ANTARCTIC CIRCLE

MAP SCALE

0   500   1000

kilometres

120°

60°

50°   130°   140°   150°   160°   170°

SOUTH